THE ECONOMICS OF THIRD WORLD MILITARY EXPENDITURE

David K. Whynes

First published 1979 by
THE MACMILLAN PRESS LTD
London and Basingstoke
Associated companies in Delhi
Dublin Hong Kong Johannesburg Lagos
Melbourne New York Singapore Tokyo

Produced by computer-controlled phototypesetting
using OCR input techniques and printed offset by
UNWIN BROTHERS LIMITED
The Gresham Press, Old Woking, Surrey
A member of the Staples Printing Group

British Library Cataloguing in Publication Data

Whynes, David K.
The economics of Third World military expenditure
    1. Underdeveloped areas — Armed Forces —
Appropriations and expenditure
    2. Underdeveloped areas — Military policy
    I. Title
355.6'22   UA17

ISBN 0-333-24346-3

For my parents

Contents

List of Tables and Figures

Preface

As far as observers of the 'developed' nations are concerned, the world has been at peace since 1945. Although a number of internal conflicts have periodically arisen within these countries, sparked off, for example, by racial tensions as in the USA or by religious differences as in Northern Ireland, international relations *between* the major military and economic powers appear to have stabilised into some degree of tolerance and peaceful coexistence. Such a description is, however, completely inappropriate for the situation in which the Third World currently finds itself; indeed, it seems fairer to say that conflict has been endemic here since the end of the Second World War. Considering only the first few months of 1978, for example, we have witnessed Israeli advances into Lebanon, the renewal of the territorial dispute between Ethiopia and Somalia and an indeterminate guerrilla war accompanying the transition of 'Rhodesia' to 'Zimbabwe'.

Given the high incidence of armed conflict within and between some of the poorest – in material terms – nations of the world, I was concerned to assess the impact of war-related expenditures on such countries' prospects for economic development. Furthermore, and on finding that such an issue raised an inescapable moral question which I resolved, not unreasonably I feel, by deciding that the allocation of a substantial volume of economic resources for the purpose of human destruction was inherently undesirable, I attempted to outline policies which might reduce the burden of military expenditure whilst still maintaining the necessary preconditions for internal and external security.

Whilst economic theory can make at least some pretence at being value-free, economic policy clearly cannot. Any such prescriptions will therefore, of necessity, have embedded within them the attitudes and prejudices of their author; and the problem is exacerbated by the fact that where one man sees liberty, another sees slavery. I hope that my

own particular beliefs are made sufficiently clear throughout the book
for readers of differing ideological persuasions to gain something from
my analyses, even if they are obliged to disagree with my recommendations. Irrespective of the validity of my own particular conclusions,
I feel that it is important that *some* recommendations are made for, as
Hilary and Steven Rose (1970) have so elegantly observed:

> It is easier to see the quagmire and the precipice than to map out in
> detail the routes by which society can skirt them. And the evils of the
> past half-century have been sufficient to warn us all of the danger of
> vision becoming nightmare, revolution bureaucracy, and the rational
> logic of science an instrument for man's destruction. That man and
> his planet survive is a continuing tribute to luck, human ingenuity
> and society's adaptive capacity. We cannot rely on the permanent
> success of this combination (pp. 271–2)

I first became interested in defence economics when I was a post-
graduate student at the University of St Andrews in 1971–2, and I
should like to thank Ranald May, Peter Robson and Keith Shaw for
their assistance in the preparation of my Master's thesis which forms
the core of the present volume. I continued working in the area whilst
at the University of York where, again, many friends and colleagues
were forthcoming with advice and encouragement. In particular, I
should like to thank Stephanie Stray, John Suckling and Arthur Walker.
Nottingham has proved to be a fertile environment for writing, and
I should wish to express my appreciation to colleagues and students for
their tolerance regarding my continual absences whilst working on the
book. In particular, Yvonne C. Rogers has contributed in many respects,
not the least being her preparation of the typescript despite the vagaries
of influenza. Roger Bowles patiently read the entire manuscript whilst,
I am sure, disagreeing with the larger part of it, and gently persuaded
me to turn my farrago of 'ongoing and meaningful situations' into
sensible economics – the fact that many such obfuscations remain
should be interpreted as a tribute to my stubbornness and not to any
deficiencies on his or, for that matter, anyone else's, part.
Finally, my thanks to the following for permission to use tables and
data: the International Peace Research Institute, Stockholm; the International Institute for Strategic Studies, London; the Arms Control and
Disarmament Agency, Washington; the Centre for Afro-Asian
Research, Budapest. On a point of style, and given the proliferation of

American literature in the field, I have followed the convention of referring to 'one thousand million' as 'one billion'.

D.K.W.

April 1978

Abbreviations

EIU	*Economist Intelligence Unit (UK)*
IISS	*International Institute for Strategic Studies (UK)*
LPDSG	*Labour Party Defence Study Group (UK)*
MEADP	*Ministry of Economic Affairs and Development Planning (Tanzania)*
NACLA	*North American Congress on Latin America (USA)*
NEDC	*National Economic Development Council (UK)*
SIPRI	*Stockholm International Peace Research Institute (Sweden)*
UN	*United Nations (USA)*
USACDA	*United States Arms Control and Disarmament Agency (USA)*

1 Introduction

Even though the military could find that its claim to be the 'world's oldest profession' has been pre-empted by an altogether different type of occupation, it must surely rank as one of the most ancient of social institutions. Indeed, history attests to the fact that every nation, society or culture has possessed some form of institutionalised arrangement whereby resources may be mobilised for the purpose of perpetrating and resisting aggression. In earliest times, the military institution was clearly informal and, in the context of tribal living, it might have consisted of nothing more than a tacit understanding on the part of the members that they were required to take up arms should the interests of the tribe be threatened.

As far as the Western experience is concerned, the first recognisable formal military institution was probably the Roman Army of some two millennia ago. Developing from the conscripted citizen militia, the Roman armed forces became highly professionalised, that is, the job of the soldier now became a full-time occupation as a career and discipline hierarchy became established. Furthermore, the maintenance of such a military became the responsibility of the Roman citizenry who contributed to the defence budget in the form of taxation.

Although the history of various armed forces has taken some strange twists since the Roman period, these basic features of professionalism remain recognisable in most armed forces throughout the world today. Indeed, from an organisational point of view, there has been little change in the nature of the military institution, although Caesar's ghost is probably continually surprised by the acceleration of military technology and the tendency of modern military administrations to be slightly less confident about the positive correlation between military ability and wealth.

Given the long history of the military institution as a recipient of public funds, we might well be led to believe that the defence sector was likely to be a well-researched area as far as economics is concerned. With a few notable exceptions, however, this is not the case.

One of the earliest, and certainly one of the most erudite, treatments of defence by an economist is to be found in Adam Smith's *Wealth of Nations*, which first appeared in 1776. The final third of this volume is devoted to an analysis of public finance and, in this context, Smith declared that the provision of national defence from public funds was the 'first duty of the sovereign'. In common with many of Smith's arguments, this proposition was proved by recourse to historical evidence. Amongst 'nations of shepherds', Smith argued, soldiering will be an activity carried out by all as the need arises, this being feasible as the methods of warfare in such circumstances were supposedly unsophisticated. However, as the art of war, 'the noblest of all arts', evolved, such a casual military organisation was no longer possible for two major reasons. First, wars become more protracted, implying that soldiers could no longer provide for themselves whilst campaigning. Secondly, the technology of warfare developed and thus put the costs of weaponry beyond the reach of individuals' incomes. Furthermore, in line with an important theme throughout Smith's book, division of labour and specialisation in the military profession would inevitably lead to greater effectiveness.

Smith concluded that, as nations became 'civilised', provision had to be made for the creation of a public defence force. This could take the form of either a conscripted militia, such as those then employed by the Arabs and Tartars, or a professional standing army, manned by volunteers and based on the Roman model or that of the army of Peter the Great in Russia. Of these two alternatives, Smith believed that history proved the latter to be the most effective. Indeed, he concluded with the assertion that 'civilisation' could only be protected by means of a standing army; furthermore, he added that it was only by means of the use of a professional armed force that 'a barbarous country' could be 'suddenly and tolerably civilised'.[1]

These arguments of Smith, themselves an extension of the earlier Platonic model of efficiency via specialisation, effectively formed the corpus of economists' contributions to defence analysis until relatively recently. Why has this been so?

From the point of view of the economist, the prevaling methodology of the nineteenth and early-twentieth centuries was hardly conducive to defence analysis. Central to this methodology was the concern with the allocation of resources by means of a competitive market process within the context of a political and social consensus. Factors indirectly related to the equilibria of supplies and demands, such as the distribution of wealth and power, were considered to be peripheral to the economist's interests and were to be regarded as 'givens'. In fact, they were best left to other species of social scientists although, even within these disciplines, conflict and violence were seldom regarded as 'proper' areas of study as they were at odds with the prevailing orthodoxy of liberal democracy.[2]

A more concrete problem for the economist in particular was, of course, the paucity and inaccuracy of data. An important ingredient in military strategy is secrecy and researchers accordingly found themselves frustrated in their search for 'hard' facts to substantiate those theories which they were able to develop.

Since the Second World War, considerable advances have been made and defence economics has begun to emerge from its obscurity. Indeed, there are a number of reasons to explain the increasing attention being paid to the area. First, economists have come to realise that, in some respects, the activities of individual actors within an economy, such as firms or consumers, may be analysed in a similar manner to nations competing in an international context, and the analyses of 'strategies' via 'game theory' has led to a changing attitude towards both economics and defence studies. Secondly, economists have become increasingly aware of the problems of the limited perspective entailed by the traditional methodology. This has led, in particular, to a dismantling of former barriers erected between economics and other disciplines such as law, politics, the natural sciences and also defence studies, and a heightened understanding of more general issues has been permitted. Thirdly, the growth of the public sector in capitalist societies has forced economists to develop explanations of economic phenomena without recourse to market or competitive models, In parallel with a growing interest in defence, therefore, health care and education are now regarded as 'legitimate' areas within the wider body of the economics discipline. Finally, to the joy of the statistically-minded, estimates of military spending have become more widely available, and the empirical testing of economic propositions regarding the defence sector is now more feasible.

A complementary factor in the long stagnation of defence analysis was the attitude of the military profession itself. Traditionally, the senior officers of the armed forces enjoyed complete freedom in the determination of resource mobilisation for war purposes whilst, for their part, economists were content to defer to such 'political' decisions and simply calculate the requirements of the military's preferred strategy. However, the escalating costs of defence led many countries, especially the UK and USA in the late-1950s, to conceed that Clemenceau might have been correct in his assertion that war was far too serious a business to be left to the generals. Economic appraisal was accordingly introduced into the defence budgetary system, serving to stimulate the interest of both economists and strategists in one another's fields. As a result of this cross-fertilisation, the past two decades have seen the publication of several important studies of particular aspects of defence economics, and we shall be referring to these at a later stage.

The particular area of the general field of 'defence economics' chosen for the present enquiry is the military expenditure of the Third World. Although we shall be concerned primarily with *economic* implications of expenditures, we shall naturally consider social, political and strategic factors in addition, as the military phenomenon will be shown to have implications for all of these. Before going further, we must clarify our declaration of intent and, to do this, it is convenient to 'dismember' the title.

Third World. The term 'Third World' is simply a convenient label to embrace those nations not formally part of the 'First' and 'Second' worlds, these being made up of the capitalist West and the socialist East, although the relative ranking will depend upon the political opinions of the observer. Clearly, the concept of a Third World nation is better sensed than defined and this is unfortunately true of a number of other classifications of nations which have been devised.

The favourite distinction of the economist is that between 'developed country' (DC) and 'developing' or 'less-developed countries' (LDC), and the nations included in these two groups display a marked correlation with those derived from the previous classification. Generally, it is the value of per capita national income or gross national product (GNP) which serves as the criterion for distinguishing DCs from LDCs, but it is argued that additional factors, such as the nature of production, style of living, political institutions and so forth, must also be taken into account. For these reasons therefore, Kuwait is usually considered to be 'developing', despite its vast income.

Other social science disciplines have discovered their own ways of distinguishing between nations. Sociologists, for example, might talk of a progressive shift from 'folk' to 'urban' culture during the development process, whilst political scientists could see such development in terms of political maturation. One final way of sub-dividing the world, and a method of great significance for our purpose, is in terms of military alliances. The First and Second worlds are, in fact, virtually equivalent to the two major defensive alliances, the Warsaw Treaty Organisation (WTO) and the North Atlantic Treaty Organisation (NATO).[3]

Owing to the diversity of potential definitions of our subject area, we are forced to be somewhat arbitrary. For the purpose of our analyses, we shall employ the term 'DC' to describe each member country of NATO and WTO, as well as the remaining states of Europe, Oceania and Japan. The Third World, or the 'LDC' group, is defined as that which remains. In addition, it will be necessary to sub-divide the LDC group itself into regions, and the composition of these will be made clear in the next chapter.

Military. The definition of the 'military' or 'defence sector' of the economy is also somewhat ambiguous. In some countries, for example, this sector might include the police forces or, as in the case of China, a citizen militia. In general, we shall use this term to refer to a nation's standing army, including a navy and air force where appropriate. Also included are security forces and the defence administration, where these are financed by state expenditure. The militaries which concern us are those considered 'legitimate', constitutionally subservient to, or standing in place of, civil government, and to which a proportion of public funds is devoted. This definition implies that we wish to make no distinction at this stage between the civil state, which maintains a military force as part of its public sector programme, and the military regime, which arises as a result of a coup or some other seizure of power and state control by the leaders of the armed forces. As we shall see, there is not a great deal to be gained from distinguishing between the economic effects of these two.

With some exceptions, we shall only be concerned with the armed forces in times of peace, in the sense that no external or internal wars will be in process at the time in question. The role of the military will therefore have more facets than those entailed by the purely strategic function (national defence and offence), and it is just these facets which will come in for the closest scrutiny. This imposed condition precludes the possibility of the discussion of the temporary (or guerrilla) army, composed of non-professionals, and also of the foreign army, made up either of mercenaries or of international peace-keeping forces. Such armies generally come into being during periods of warfare and social disintegration. Our analysis on the other hand is aimed primarily at the economic effects of expenditure in a stable, or at least semi-stable, situation.

Expenditure. The military 'expenditures' to be considered in these analyses are essentially those resources devoted to defence by the public expenditure budget of the country concerned. This definition is therefore contingent upon the previously-adopted definition of the 'military'. An additional classification of defence spending which will be used is that of 'major weapons' – aircraft, shipping, missiles and land vehicles – as these items form the basis of many sets of military statistics.

The proportion of annual military expenditure allocated by *all* LDC nations amounts to around one-quarter of the world total, an amount corresponding to slightly less than the individual contributions of the USA or the Warsaw Treaty Organisation. When compared with the resource commitments of these 'superpowers', the expenditure of any one LDC appears quite insignificant and we are therefore prompted to ask – why should the Third World be singled out for special treatment in a book such as the present one? This question may be answered by considering three simple propositions.

First, the provision of defence by any one country represents an economic (or 'opportunity') cost to that country, in that resources so expended cannot then be made available for the production of other commodities. In practical terms, this means that more military expenditure precludes the production of more health care, railways, bread or steel (assuming that all other things remain equal); similarly, more of the latter implies less of the former. When a society makes a decision to expand any one economic sector (including defence), it must accordingly evaluate the anticipated gains from that sector with respect to the opportunities forgone by the corresponding neglect of the remaining sectors.

Our second proposition is that the nations of the Third World, in spite of their individualities in terms of race, religion and culture, are united by one common factor.

No matter whether they are called 'underdeveloped', 'economically backward', or – to be more hopeful – 'emergent' or 'aspiring' countries, they are still poor countries. These countries are designated 'poor' because they are at the bottom of a ranking of countries of the world by per capita income. Alternatively they could just as readily be

labelled 'poor' in terms of non-monetary indicators, such as quality
of diet, housing, transportation, health, and education. (Meier, 1970,
p. 3)

The definition of this poverty which unites the Third World nations is,
of course, imprecise, as it is dependent upon the particular beliefs and
prejudices of the observer. However, most would surely accept the
following facts as being representative of Third World poverty in some
general sense – life expectancy in Japan is twice that in Nigeria; in
Mali, around 80 per cent of the population is totally illiterate; the
average daily protein intake of North Americans is twice that of the
people of India; per capita expenditure on health care in the UK is over
one hundred times that for Ethiopia; the per capita income in Malawi
is less than one-sixtieth of that of the USA.[4]
Our third proposition is simply a restatement of the economist's
fundamental value-judgement, namely, 'more is preferred' or 'poverty
is sub-optimal'. We should therefore think it reasonable for LDCs to
attempt to implement development programmes in an effort to alleviate
their present conditions and recent data provide tangible, although
superficial, evidence of some improvement. Over the period 1971–76,
the average annual growth rate of Third World GNP was 5.3 per cent
which, if deflated by the population growth rate of 2.1 per cent, implies
a healthy overall annual increase in per capita incomes of around 3 per
cent. Indeed, the figure for petroleum exporters was even higher.
However, it is the composition of this aggregate growth which really
indicates the true situation. Whilst the expansion rate of organised
manufacturing was 7.3 per cent, the average growth of agricultural
output was 2.4 per cent each year. With the exception of a few of the
richer LDCs, it is the agricultural sector which is the main component
of LDC economic activity and, therefore, the key determinant of the
living standards of the mass of the population in the Third World. The
data therefore suggest that the expansion of agriculture has only just
kept pace with population growth and it would appear that, in general,
government economic policy in the Third World has been ineffectual
in producing a sustained rise in the real living standards of the population. Similarly, government policy to tackle problems such as disease,
illiteracy and urban unemployment has, as yet, touched only the tip of
the iceberg.
In addition to the manufacturing sector, another major growth area
has been defence. For the period 1970–76, the annual LDC military
allocation increased at 6.5 per cent, or at twice the rate of growth of

per capita incomes. Furthermore, the annual average growth rate of the importation of major weapons was a staggering 16.5 per cent over the same period.[5] This progressive reallocation of resources in favour of the defence sector suggests that, in spite of their extreme poverty, the Third World nations accord defence a high priority.

Our study will therefore be concerned with trying to discover the reasons for this expansion of LDC defence in the face of poverty, the consequences of the expansion in terms of cost and security, and also the methods by which resources might be liberated from the defence sector for the relief of Third World poverty, without any necessary constraints being imposed upon military effectiveness.

The starting point for any investigation must be the actual expenditure data, and Chapter 2 reviews the material currently available. Having determined the magnitude of the problem, we then move on to a discussion of the major causes of LDC expenditure growth over the past two decades. This chapter concludes with an evaluation of the theories which relate the defence sector to overall public spending.

Chapter 3 makes an assessment of the real resource costs of military expenditure by considering those areas where the military and the civilian economy are interrelated, particular attention being paid to industrial development and manpower policies.

Chapters 4 and 5 each concern themselves with a specific defence issue of significance in a Third World context. First, the rapid growth of military aid and trade in defence equipment is examined, and cost estimates are made to parallel those of Chapter 3. Secondly, the effect of military interventions and regimes is analysed, in relation to the likely effects that such forms of government might have on defence spending and economic development in general.

The conclusions of Chapters 3 to 5 suggest that current levels of defence expenditure impose considerable economic and social costs onto the Third World, and Chapter 6 appraises several possibilities for cost reduction. Finally, Chapter 7 presents some concluding reflections on the topic as a whole.

2 The Growth of Military Expenditure

The opening section of the discussion is devoted to an examination of the raw materials of the analysis – expenditure and related data for nations and regions throughout the world. We must be clear from the outset, however, that the analysis of military data can only be undertaken with a number of reservations borne firmly in mind.

Of all social science data, it is probably that of the defence sector which is the most scarce and/or unreliable, and the reason for this is obvious. In a situation of potential or actual conflict, a knowledge of one's defence capabilities, in terms of resource allocation, is clearly of strategic value to one's potential or actual enemies. The declaration by NATO, for example, of a massive expenditure programme for tactical nuclear weapons would tell WTO a considerable amount about NATO's concept of strategy. By appealing to the requirement of national security, many governments therefore fail to publish data, or present information in such a manner as to disguise the true magnitude or purpose of the resources committed.

In spite of the problems outlined above, it is generally possible for outside observers to make estimates of the form and volume of military spending currently being undertaken. The quality of such estimates, however, is a function of the type of expenditure being observed. Whilst we could be reasonably confident, for example, of an estimate of the number of warships owned by a particular navy (as they would be so readily observable), it is a completely different matter to make inferences about, say, the number of light machine-guns or rounds of ammunition carried by particular battalions. This is simply due to the relatively large numbers of minor items which are employed, and also to the respective ease of concealment. On the manpower side, estimation might also be rendered difficult owing to military organisation. The distinction between soldiers, police and para-military forces is very unclear in many

9

instances, and the existence of 'part-time' soldiers in a number of countries is an additional complicating factor.[1] Concerning trade, it is frequently difficult to distinguish between resources allocated for domestic use and those used to purchase imported weapons. In general, consistency is therefore difficult to achieve.

However, even if estimates are made, the actual process is clearly time-consuming; indeed, this is true for most economic data series. The social scientist is therefore often obliged to work with out-of-date material, producing hypotheses which might already have been disproved by immediate events. In working with UN data, for example, one would have to go back to around the year 1970 in order to obtain a full international sample of LDCs for comparative analysis.

The problem of international consistency in statistics is also encountered when dealing with associated data, such as that for population and national income. As yet, there is no agreed international standard for classification and measurement, with the result that comparison of countries in these terms might also be somewhat suspect.[2]

The two principal sources for military data are the International Peace Research Institute in Stockholm (SIPRI) and the International Institute for Strategic Studies, London (IISS). Throughout the present text, use will be made of data from both these sources, although it must be pointed out that each of these organisations employs its own measurement convention. Estimates, therefore, might not be mutually consistent in all aspects, although the general trends will be common.[3]

Such difficulties notwithstanding, an examination of the evidence is important for it does provide the empirical basis of our understanding of the economics of defence spending. Having presented such data, the present chapter then goes on to advance reasons for the expenditure trends and ultimately relates them to general theories of public expenditure.

TABLE 2.1   Share of Annual World Military Expenditure expressed as a percentage of world total (constant prices and exchange rates)

	1952	1956	1960	1964	1968	1972	1976
NATO	66	64	63	56	56	48	45
WTO	26	22	23	26	26	28	26
Third World	5	11	12	16	16	21	26

Source: Derived from Barnaby and Huisken (1975), Table 1, p. 8; SIPRI (1977), Table 7A1, p. 222–3.

TABLE 2.2　Indices of Military Expenditure by Region, 1960–76, (1960 = 100: constant prices and exchange rates)

	1961	1962	1963	1964	1965	1966	1967	1968	1969	1970	1971	1972	1973	1974	1975	1976
NATO	104	113	113	111	111	125	140	142	137	129	124	126	123	123	122	125
WTO	124	137	150	144	139	145	157	182	194	198	199	200	201	200	200	202
Middle East	107	119	133	154	177	211	276	332	383	461	479	658	856	1174	1483	1630
South Asia	106	137	213	210	217	212	193	200	212	220	262	284	255	240	257	294
Far East	104	111	116	126	141	144	158	176	189	205	225	237	238	243	244	256
China	117	136	153	182	192	216	216	226	244	269	279	270	270	270	270	270
Africa	147	221	246	297	339	354	439	509	609	645	712	736	794	943	1167	1333
Latin America	99	102	106	106	122	125	145	142	147	151	170	174	183	166	213	207
WORLD	109	120	125	125	126	138	152	160	163	161	166	163	163	166	170	175

Source: Derived from SIPRI (1977), Table 7A1, p. 222–3.

Over the past two decades, the annual total of military expenditures undertaken by the nations of the world has doubled and now stands in excess of $310 thousand million dollars each year (which, incidentally represents around $10,000 every second).[4] Table 2.1 illustrates the basic breakdown of this total between the three main world groupings – NATO, WTO and the Third World. As may be seen, in the early 1950s NATO accounted for two-thirds of the world's annual defence budget. However, at the present time, this share has been eroded to less than one half, primarily by the increase in expenditures of the countries of the Third World. The proportion of WTO has remained constant at around one quarter.

This expanding share of the Third World countries obviously arises because of their relatively high expenditure growth rates. As may be seen from Table 2.2, however, growth in the Third World has been far from uniform. Although all of the LDC regions show an average annual growth in excess of that of NATO, WTO and the world total, two regions in particular stand out. Whilst most areas have doubled or trebled their budgets, Africa and the Middle East have increased their annual allocations thirteen- and sixteen-fold respectively.[5] Also, with two exceptions, all regions have increased their expenditure annually; these exceptions are South Asia in the late 1960s and NATO in the late 1960s/early 1970s. Indeed, in constant price terms, NATO is currently spending less than it was in 1968.

Whilst the first two tables concern themselves with larger areas, Table 2.3 presents more detailed information for 91 major nations listed according to the regional groupings of Table 2.2. This table presents estimates of annual defence spending for the most recent data available (July 1977) and relates it to a number of other key economic indicators. The indicators presented include population and per capita income, the defence 'burden' (i.e. the proportion of total national income devoted to the military sector) and the per capita income and defence expenditure annual growth rates. These rates are derived from data for the past five years and, as they are estimated in current prices, make no allowances for inflation. For this reason, care should be taken when attempting international comparisons.

Although the analysis of this material will be left until later in the chapter, a few general observations are worth making at this point. As may be clearly seen, the expenditure of the USA, the USSR and, to some extent, China are of a completely different order from the expenditures of other nations, and it is such expenditure magnitudes which cause these nations to be labelled the 'superpowers'. Over 62 per

TABLE 2.3   Defence Expenditure and Related Data for 91 Countries, 1977, in current prices and exchange rates. Growth rates calculated over the past five years. 'n.a.' indicates data are unavailable

Country	Defence Expend- iture ($m)	Popula- tion (m)	Per capita income ($)	Defence/ GNP (%)	Annual per capita Income Growth (%)	Annual Defence Expend- iture Growth (%)
USA	109700	217	7798	6.5	9.3	6.5
Belgium	1820	10	6704	2.7	16.6	16.4
Britain	10880	57	3966	4.8	10.2	5.8
Canada	3610	23	7501	2.1	12.9	13.9
Denmark	1080	5	6718	3.2	13.5	17.4
France	11720	54	6568	3.3	14.0	8.4
German FR	13760	63	7110	3.1	13.3	5.6
Greece	1100	9	2502	4.8	16.2	17.4
Italy	4640	57	2850	2.9	7.0	4.0
Luxembourg	25	0.4	6760	1.0	15.7	13.8
Netherlands	3360	14	6101	3.9	16.4	12.4
Norway	1120	4	7645	3.6	19.3	13.9
Portugal	461	9	1798	2.9	18.8	2.1
Turkey	2650	41	978	6.6	23.8	34.4
USSR	127000	258	3878	12.7	22.0	11.2
Bulgaria	538	9	2389	2.5	16.9	15.6
Czechoslovakia	1610	15	3057	3.5	7.9	4.8
German DR	2890	17	2780	6.0	7.6	9.2
Hungary	590	11	2189	2.6	10.6	−4.0
Poland	2440	35	1968	3.6	10.6	7.9
Romania	824	22	2097	1.8	13.4	11.8
Albania	137	3	415	12.5	−1.1	3.8
Austria	534	8	5051	1.3	16.7	16.3
Eire	146	3	2531	1.8	7.8	13.5
Finland	426	5	6837	1.3	26.4	16.5
Spain	2150	36	2794	2.1	20.4	17.4
Sweden	2830	8	9258	3.7	15.7	10.7
Switzerland	1280	7	8764	2.2	16.8	12.5
Yugoslavia	1640	22	1389	5.4	22.8	18.7
Australia	2800	14	7198	2.8	21.1	15.5
Japan	6100	114	4973	1.1	13.8	14.7
New Zealand	211	3	3925	1.7	8.1	4.7
Egypt	4370	39	332	33.9	12.1	25.9
Iran	7900	35	1634	13.9	35.1	40.8
Iraq	1660	12	1203	11.7	36.7	48.9

Country	Defence Expenditure ($m)	Population (m)	Per capita income ($)	Defence/ GNP (%)	Annual per capita Income Growth (%)	Annual Defence Expenditure Growth (%)
Israel	4270	4	3479	33.9	12.7	30.5
Jordan	201	3	450	15.4	13.9	13.9
Kuwait	2060	1	11560	16.3	n.a.	n.a.
Lebanon	70	3	1241	1.9	18.7	−1.7
Saudi Arabia	7530	8	4960	20.2	68.2	62.1
Syria	1070	8	606	22.8	20.8	49.2
N. Yemen	60	7	119	7.2	15.9	46.6
S. Yemen	44	2	279	8.7	32.8	29.6
Bangladesh	52	81	66	1.0	9.3	−5.7
Afghanistan	48	20	65	3.7	−5.7	7.7
India	3650	622	144	3.8	7.9	9.7
Pakistan	819	74	136	8.1	17.0	17.3
Sri Lanka	48	15	191	1.7	5.3	13.7
Burma	113	32	83	4.2	n.a.	5.6
Taiwan	1000	17	934	6.2	9.9	9.3
Indonesia	1350	136	215	4.6	27.6	47.3
N. Korea	1000	17	532	11.2	22.9	12.7
S. Korea	1800	35	523	9.8	16.4	39.4
Laos	27	4	60	12.8	−2.5	12.3
Malaysia	544	13	645	6.3	12.4	17.3
Mongolia	121	2	1824	4.3	29.6	29.8
Philippines	419	45	364	2.5	15.6	44.9
Singapore	340	2	2778	5.2	23.3	8.1
Thailand	639	45	326	4.3	13.2	21.5
China	26000	925	334	8.4	n.a.	21.3
Algeria	387	18	811	2.7	23.3	40.3
Libya	229	3	4639	1.9	21.6	12.1
Ethiopia	103	29	99	3.6	6.1	26.4
Ghana	131	10	346	3.6	1.4	43.9
Kenya	35	14	195	1.3	n.a.	n.a.
Morocco	346	18	431	4.4	12.1	29.4
Nigeria	2400	66	366	9.9	30.1	77.5
Rhodesia	159	7	504	4.7	17.3	49.3
Senegal	47	5	259	3.9	n.a.	n.a.
Somalia	25	3	90	8.3	10.3	21.7

Country	Defence Expend- iture ($m)	Popula- tion (m)	Per capita income ($)	Defence/ GNP (%)	Annual per capita Income Growth (%)	Annual Defence Expend- iture Growth (%)
S. Africa	1900	27	1178	6.0	6.1	27.6
Sudan	131	19	150	4.7	7.7	−2.1
Tanzania	70	16	119	3.7	3.1	8.0
Tunisia	156	6	792	3.3	20.3	52.7
Uganda	49	12	163	2.5	5.0	16.7
Zaire	77	26	133	2.2	9.0	−2.2
Zambia	309	5	478	12.4	n.a.	n.a.
Argentina	1420	26	2000	2.7	0.9	12.4
Bolivia	74	6	423	3.0	14.1	30.2
Brazil	2070	113	1157	1.6	23.3	17.0
Chile	614	11	823	6.8	1.7	37.1
Colombia	140	26	578	0.9	15.3	11.1
Cuba	290	10	470	6.4	−2.0	n.a.
Dominican Rep.	43	5	805	1.1	17.6	7.0
Ecuador	114	8	612	2.4	21.9	23.5
Honduras	25	3	333	2.3	n.a.	n.a.
Mexico	543	64	1446	0.6	18.3	11.4
Paraguay	36	3	614	2.1	21.6	17.4
Peru	406	17	633	3.8	7.3	14.0
Uruguay	75	3	1115	2.1	9.1	−0.7
Venezuela	513	13	2549	1.6	25.1	12.1

Source: Derived from IISS (various dates), The Military Balance.

cent of NATOs budget comes from the USA, whilst the USSR con- tributes 85 per cent to the total WTO spending; these two countries in other words, account for 50 per cent of global military expenditure.[6]

If we consider LDC expenditure by region in Table 2.3, we find that Latin America and Africa each total around $6–7000 million in annual defence spending and, bearing in mind the extraordinary growth rate of the African total and the relatively slow rate for Latin America, it is clear that African military budgets must have started from a very low figure in the early 1960s. The total for South Asia is a little lower than the previous figure, whilst that of the Far East is somewhat larger, although the exclusion of Vietnam from the table suggests that this total is a considerable underestimate. Of the greatest importance, however, is the Middle Eastern total which, at around $30,000 million, exceeds the sum of the previous four regional totals.

THE CAUSES OF GROWTH

The evidence presented in the preceeding section attests to a significant growth in military expenditure in most of the major nations of the world. Whilst, in many cases, this growth is similar to, or smaller than, the growth in income, there are other instances where military growth far outstrips income growth, and casual inspection suggests that most of the examples of the latter are LDCs. Indeed, particularly extreme cases inlude Israel, Syria, Sri Lanka, S. Korea, Morocco, S. Africa, Tunisia, Uganda and Bolivia. In the following section, we shall attempt to isolate the causes of such expenditure trends.

The rationale for defence expenditure, and the reasons for its growth, can be summarised as follows:

  (i) security
 (ii) internal repression
(iii) the inefficiencies of the budgetary process
 (iv) the existence of a military-industrial complex
  (v) the vested interests of the military establishment
 (vi) the needs of ideology and national identity
(vii) imperialism

Whilst some factors in this list are complete explanations of defence spending, others simply modify the level which would be predicted, other things being equal. Any, some or all might therefore be appropriate in any particular instance of expenditure growth. To facilitate exposition, we shall deal with each factor individually.

Security.   The growth of the military sector is ultimately bound up with warfare and strategy, so that any discussion of the former presupposes analysis of the latter. From the point of view of strategy, perhaps the most fundamental contribution to the theory of warfare is that of Clausewitz whose book, *Vom Kriege*, first appeared in 1832. Axiomatic to his analysis is the notion of the sovereign state, recognising no authority beyond its own. One of the primary objectives of such a state is the increase of its own power at the expense of others, the logical implication of such a postulate being the existence of perennial interstate conflict. Resolution therefore occurs only when one state succeeds in imposing its will upon another. We conclude that warfare is a rational extension of international politics and is waged to achieve a desired goal, the conquest or control of rival states. Decisions relating to the undertaking of a war should be made in the light of the potential benefits of the goal and the costs of its achievement. In sum, war is endemic to a world composed of discrete and self conscious states.[7]

Modern theorists, such as Aron and Kahn, have altered the historical perspectives of Clausewitz' analysis, but not its practical implications. In the contemporary world, conflicts do exist which cannot be resolved by recourse to 'normal politics'. Given the fact that war cannot be universally outlawed and that international law is impotent without a supranational enforcement agency, armed conflicts are inevitable. Furthermore, the currently dominant ideology of national political sovereignty has given inter-state warfare an eschatological status. The resultant effects are (i) the accumulation of military equipment for offensive purposes, and (ii) the accumulation of military equipment for defensive purposes, should an offensive from without be anticipated.[8] A substantial proportion of the growth trend previously observed can be explained in terms of these strategic necessities. For example, in the early 1950s, the US defence commitment rose owing to the Korean war, and the subsequent growth in expenditure can be interpreted as a desire for insurance against attack from other economic systems, regarded by the USA as potential threats to national security. As McNamara, the former US Secretary of Defence, observed:

> We cannot for a moment afford to relax our vigilance against a possible Soviet first strike. But our greatest deterrent against such a strike is not a massive, costly and highly penetrable ABM [anti-ballistic missile] shield, but a fully credible, offensive, assured-destruction capability. (McNamara, 1968, p. 166)

Doubtless, McNamara's Soviet counterpart was thinking along similar lines.

Amongst the nations of the Third World, the point is most easily made with respect to the Middle East and the Far East. Since the early 1950s, the conflicts in these areas have risen to the status of major wars and, in fact, these regions are major contributors to the rise in LDC military expenditure in recent years.

With the benefit of hindsight, it can now be seen that the Middle East has always been a potential flashpoint for violence. Given that the Jewish people desired to create and defend a homeland in the very centre of the Arab world, it is perhaps not suprising that major conflicts occurred in 1948/49, 1956 and 1967. Throughout this period, both Arabs and Israelis progressively expanded their defence budgets but it was Israel's strategic and economic superiority (and US aid) which, in the last instance, brought them a crushing victory in a matter of days. The net result was substantial territorial gains at the expense of Egypt, Syria and Jordan.

After this 'Six Day War', both sides commenced an accelerated armaments drive and, as well as expanding domestic budgets, placed progressively more reliance upon weapon imports. Initially through Nasser, Egypt had developed a trading relationship with the USSR and several billion dollars' worth of armaments had been purchased on favourable terms by the early 1970s.[9] Syria too was receiving Soviet assistance, some of which was passed on to Jordan. Israel, in turn, looked towards the USA for a parallel influx of sophisticated weaponry, such as fighter aircraft.

For the next six years, the conflict was characterised by perpetual skirmishing rather than full-scale confrontation as both sides tested one another's strengths. Year by year, the defence burden increased. In 1973, however, the Arab nations engineered a simultaneous advance on both the Egyptian and the Syrian fronts and they succeeded in winning a substantial psychological victory over Israeli invincibility, despite little tangible gain.

A position of conflict and stalemate has therefore existed in the Middle East for some ten years and this has entailed enormous sacrifices for the nations involved. At the end of 1977, President Sadat of Egypt initiated peace overtures towards Israel although it remains to be seen whether Israel or the remaining Arab allies will find a settlement acceptable.

In spite of its importance, the Arab-Israeli conflict is not the sole cause of military escalation in the Middle East. Until agreement was reached in 1975, Iran and Iraq experienced escalation owing to Iranian support for Kurdish secessionist movement in Iraq. A number of the smaller oil-states, such as Kuwait and Bahrain, have also increased their expenditures for fear of possible interference in their affairs.

Like the Middle East, the Far East has experienced warfare since the end of the Second World War. The conflicts of the 1950s involved the Korean theatre and also the anti-colonial struggle of Vietnam against the French. During the 1960s, the Vietnamese theatre expanded to include neighbouring states and most significantly, substantial American involvement. It is this latter factor, of course, which goes a long way towards explaining the rise in NATO expenditure during the mid-1960s and the subsequent decline with US withdrawal.

Africa's high rate of growth since the late 1950s may be attributed to the fact that many African nations gained their independence at about this time. Prior to independence, colonies had been defended by small units, led by ex-patriates, which served few strategic functions other than the provision of a tangible illustration of imperial rule.[10] With the departure of the colonial powers, the new states felt it desirable to establish their own defence services for the purposes of national security. This process was considered particularly urgent for a number of reasons, the most obvious being that the ex-colonial forces as they then stood were considered inadequate to serve any meaningful strategic function. This factor was also important in other ex-colonies throughout the world.

In addition, there has been a growing fear in sub-Saharan Africa of the increasing military might of the 'white enclaves' – Rhodesia and South Africa. In parallel, the annual defence expenditures of these latter nations has also been rising, one causal factor being the uncertainty attached to the possible future intentions of newly-independent 'black' African states. This circular causation has produced a rise in South African defence spending from $US 61.6 million in 1960 to $US 229.2 million in 1965.[11] There does exist another important reason for the rise in South African expenditures and this will be discussed in the next section.

Border disputes have been relatively common in Africa, owing to social and racial tensions and disagreements over national boundaries. To some extent, this may be seen as a consequence of the colonial legacy of arbitrary territorial compartmentalisation, which has also brought about conflicts within states and demands for recognition by ethnic sub-states. Naturally, any such conflict will require increased expenditure on defence, and also for the policing of national boundaries. Examples of border disputes are the Morocco/Algeria conflict (1963/67), Somalia and Ethiopia (regularly since the early 1960s), Kenya and Somalia (1963–67), and the frequent minor disputes between Uganda and Tanzania. Several major internal struggles have occurred – Zaire (throughout the 1960s) the North/South conflict in the Sudan (1965–69), Rwanda (1963–64). Ethiopia (throughout the 1970s), Angola and Mozambique (mid-1970s) and Nigeria (1967–71). The Nigerian civil war in particular had a great influence upon African defence spending, and its occurrence goes a long way in explaining the rise and subsequent fall of expenditure.

India's defence budget has continued to expand, again due to internal and external conflicts. Examples include the Goa (1961) and Mizos (1966–67) separationist attempts, border disputes with China (1962), and the conflicts with Pakistan (1965 and the early 1970s). Indian defence is also expanding as a reaction to Chinese increases – other aspects of these nations expenditure patterns will be examined subsequently.

It is only in Latin America that we find expenditure growth rates on par with those encountered amongst the DCs. One reason for this fact is that the armed forces of the region are long-established and have expanded slowly over a considerable period of time, rather than abruptly as in the case of Africa. The Latin American states also tend to possess a certain stability, at least in respect of aggression from neighbours or from the rest of the world. What might be considered surprising about Latin American trends is the fact that the governments of the region are predominantly military, this having led some observers to anticipate heavy spending on the military sector. Again, we shall examine this issue in a later chapter.

Internal repression. We argued above that military expenditure is motivated by the desire to ensure the geographical sovereignty of the nation, in terms of attempts at conquest from without and attempts at separation from within. However, the military is also an important force in the maintenance of political sovereignty within a country. Paul Baran (1957) was convinced that the arms build-up in LDCs was not primarily due to the fear of external aggression and the need for geographical unity.

> The conclusion is inescapable that the prodigious waste of the underdeveloped countries' resources on vast military establishments is *not* dictated by the existence of an *external* danger. The atmosphere of such a danger is merely created and recreated in order to facilitate the existence of comprador regimes in these countries, and the armed forces that they maintain are needed primarily, if not exclusively, for the suppression of *internal* popular movements for national and social liberation. (p. 414, original emphasis)

In the period in which Baran was writing, there did indeed seem little possibility of a major intra-Third World conflict. Recently, this pattern has clearly changed – the Middle and Far Eastern situations are obvious examples. Nevertheless, the essential point remains – that military expenditure can serve a counter-revolutionary purpose.

A number of LDCs are characterised by factors which make this issue particularly relevant. Firstly, they have very low levels of per capita national income, implying that a significant quantity of investment resources for development is unlikely to arise voluntarily. Secondly, there exists a great dichotomy, in terms of the distribution of wealth, between the elite, who effectively control the means of production and who also possess the monopoly of political power, and the mass of the population.

It will therefore follow that, if the elite is to maintain its position, and possibly improve upon it, it must drain resources from the masses without exploiting them so much that revolution, and the eventual supersession of the elite, will occur. An effective solution to this problem is the employment of propaganda, minor consumption benefits and repression.

Luttwak (1968) presents such a model to explain the Duvalier regime in Haiti. The income of the masses was maintained marginally above an acceptable subsistence level, and the remainder was absorbed by taxation. The resultant revenue was then channelled into army and security services, propaganda agencies, luxury elite consumption and also into the social services, giving the impression of an improvement in the lot of the masses. Finally, a section of the budget was devoted to reinvestment for development.

This theory seems to be substantiated by the available evidence. During the late 1960s, the government of Haiti devoted over 25 per cent of its total public expenditure to defence[12] and this figure is much higher than the average Latin American allocation. It must be said however, that the case of Haiti may be regarded as exceptional in terms of the illustration of the theory. The operation was only made possible by the immense personal power of 'Papa Doc', the low level of political awareness among the population, the general air of superstition and the influence of 'Voodoo', and the loyalty of the Ton Ton Macoutes, whose ultimate survival depended upon the prestigious position of Duvalier himself. In spite of this, we may adapt the idea to shed some light on the nature of power under other regimes.

The Nkrumah era in Ghana was characterised by an attempt to produce industrial development by a heavy investment drive. This policy necessitated a considerable transfer of resources away from consumption and, in many ways, the manifestations of the process were similar to Duvalier's operations. A private army was created, responsible only to the President, and organs of propaganda flourished. We also observed a considerable amount of luxury consumption amongst the elite – the modernisation of government offices and institutions, the development of 'public image' services such as the airport and the Volta project, and also direct, personal luxuries such as Nkrumah's infamous private yacht. In the case of Ghana, however, there was substantially more orientation towards economic development and this, in fact, was one of the root causes of Nkrumah's downfall. The benefits of development were, to some extent, passed on to the mass of the population who, with the advantages accruing from the expansion of the educational system, became increasingly more critical of, and more hostile to, the government's policies. Nkrumah was unable to continue his operations with sufficient ruthlessness and, of course, had insufficient control over his regular armed forces, who were ultimately responsible for his demise.[13]

The Republic of South Africa provides the most graphic example of the expansion of defence for the purpose of internal repression. The annual domestic defence budget tripled during the 1960s and arms importation likewise grew – by the late 1960s, South Africa was purchasing more foreign arms than the nations of the rest of sub-Saharan Africa combined.[14] The growth of expenditure is explained almost totally by the existence of the repressive system of apartheid which is practised in South Africa. One factor in explaining this growth, therefore, is the desire to protect vested interests against newly-independent neighbours hostile to the apartheid regime. However, as the Minister of Defence observed in 1963, 'the first task of the defence forces is to help the police maintain law and order' (quoted by Christie 1970, p. 9). In other words, military expenditure should become a tool of the government (i) in enforcing the apartheid system, (ii) to prevent any strategic relationship from being formed between the indigenous black population and the anti-apartheid regimes elsewhere on the African continent. The success of these repressive operations is evidenced by Figure 2.1. This figure relates defence expenditure to political insurrection (demonstrations and spontaneous riots, premeditated attacks by armed groups) and to the number of repressive and politically-orientated government sanctions. The relationships are clear. In the early 1950s, popular agitation increased, as did military expenditure and sanctions, the first and last mutually provoking each other. The watershed, however, occurred in 1960, the year of the Sharpeville shootings. Agitation reached a peak, as did prohibitive legislation, and defence expenditure started on its rapid rise. It would seem to be the case that the decline in popular agitation during the 1960s is due to this growth in expenditure, and thus military power, serving to support the cumulation of government sanctions.

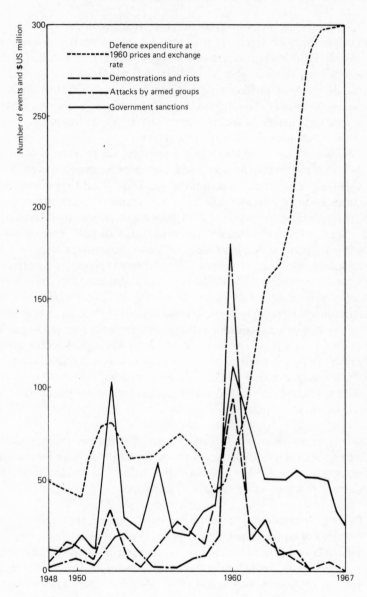

FIG. 2.1 South African Defence Expenditure and Related Political Events

Source: SIPRI (1969), p. 210–11; Taylor and Hudson (1972), pp. 88–123.

As a final element of evidence to prove that South African defence forces are intended primarily to defend against internal pressures, we need only examine the nature of the Republic's armed forces. Of the three defence services, the Army is by far the largest wing, with a particularly strong civilian militia which can be mobilised in times of national emergency. The defence forces' 'hardware' is also orientated towards anti-guerilla warfare, comprising tanks, personnel carriers, ground-attack aircraft, helicopters and so on.[15]

The role of the armed forces in the maintenance of internal political stability is most important and could, furthermore, increase even more in significance as far as the nations of the Third World are concerned. In their haste to develop, LDCs are continuously under pressure to divert more and more resources away from consumption into investment. This seems to be an economic fact which faces all LDC governments, whether despotic or benign. Indeed, it forms the basic principle of the development processes advocated by a number of theorists – for example, the planning models of Mahalanobis and popular 'critical minimum effort' thesis place great emphasis on the investment sector, with maximum absorption from surplus consumption.[16] It is clear that such a policy can only be successful with agreement on the part of the public and, ideally, this should be brought about be ideological socialisation. However, should this fail, as experience suggests it well might, a degree of threat of repression will be vital in securing adequate resource transfers. It is, of course, the armed forces alone which are capable of providing such a threat.

The budgetary process.   In the absence of a market mechanism to serve as a means of allocating resources, the defence sector receives its inputs from public funds by means of the 'budget'. In its ideal form, the budgetary process can be thought of as follows:

> Defence budgeting is an organisational routine that reflects the interplay of strategic objectives and national resource constraints. As such, it is a two-tiered exercise in choice; a means of making decisions as to the resources to be devoted *to* a state's defence establishment and, on a different level, a way of deciding how these resources will be allocated *within* the defence establishment. (Burt, 1975, p. 1, original emphasis)

In pre-1960s Britain and America, and in a number of Third World nations today, the budget was, or is far from ideal. In its crudest form, the annual defence budget often consists simply of the presentation of estimates to the central government by the senior officials of each of the armed services, and the allocation of this, or of an adjusted amount by the Treasury to the service concerned. Such an allocation system clearly gives rise to a number of unfortunate consequences.

Individual chiefs of staff will naturally favour allocation to their own particular branch of the services, whilst neglecting the needs of the others. An effective, balanced military force will not therefore result. For example. the air force might favour the purchase of supersonic interceptors and neglect its role in supporting army ground operations. This factor is particularly relevant to the LDCs where total available defence resources are limited – in such a case, it is clearly vital that the armed forces be co-ordinated for maximum efficiency.

As the critics of the US budget have been keen to point out, the cost aspects of defence provision tend to be ignored completely – requirements will be stated in absolute terms, based upon the desired objectives of military officials. Given these absolute objectives, the Treasury has no rationale for deciding upon efficient allocation *vis-à-vis* other sectors of public expenditure.[17]

Efficient allocation could also be hampered by the military's lack of analysis of marginal costs. Enthoven (1963) gives the following example:

> ... suppose that the objective were to achieve an expectation of destroying 97 per cent of 100 targets, using missiles having a 50 per cent single-shot kill probability. The requirements study would conclude that 500 missiles were required, without pointing out that the last 100 missiles only added an expectation of killing about three extra targets. (p. 416)

The traditional method of annual budgeting also ignores the problems of military planning. A substantial proportion of military expenditure is orientated towards longer-term investment (for example, the establishment of a defence manufacturing industry). The military officials are therefore under constant pressure to ensure a continual supply of funds over the projects' lives. Clearly, this problem is particularly prevalent in cases where the initial project costs are low, and therefore more attractive to the Treasury. In the case of the USA, a number of projects had to be cancelled, and the embodied resources therefore wasted, because completion was precluded by the limitations of subsequent budgets. In other cases, additional expenditure was granted, over and above the previous estimates, to prevent such resource wastage although at extra cost.

In his analysis of the UK system, Hartley (1974) suggests that the traditional method of defence budgeting in Britain was open to the same charges of inefficiency as in the USA case. Hartley is particularly concerned with the absence of any specifications for output, which implies that it is not possible to evaluate alternative methods of attaining the same defence objective.

From the economic point of view, these new systems of defence budgeting are extremely significant in view of their potential for a more rational allocation of resources, as Hartley has shown. At this stage, suffice it to say that, for nations still employing the traditional approach, the implications of that preceding is that defence expenditure, and its growth, can be caused by inefficiencies in the budgetary process of allocation. The military has an incentive to overstate its requirements which, in the first place, might not have been drawn up with sufficient consideration of economic factors. Furthermore, additional expenditure might be incurred to prevent cancellation of projects which, because of their inadequate initial costings, would otherwise be written off as resource losses.

The military-industrial complex.   The theory of the military-industrial complex is currently the most popular explanation for the rise in defence spending amongst the nations of the capitalist world. The theory has been expounded in a number of ways, but the fundamental framework is constructed as follows.

Axiomatic to the theory is the belief in the inherent instability and eventual collapse of the capitalist mode of production, if left to its own devices. This collapse might arise for a variety of reasons, depending upon the ideology of the observer – for the Keynesian, higher and higher incomes will fail to generate sufficient consumption to maintain output growth indefinitely; for the Marxian, the growth of output will outstrip demand owing to pressure on wages, leading to a fall in the rate of profit and a decline in accumulation and growth; for Baran and Sweezy (1968), it will become progressively more difficult to reabsorb the economic surplus, the excess of output over costs, which will entail eventual economic contraction.

Irrespective of the reason for the stagnation of the capitalist economies, the state in question will find it necessary to inject resources into the system in order to prevent its decline. Given that the consumers and investors have no incentive to act, public resources must be used.

The military sector is ideal for such use as a fiscal regulator for several reasons. First, it possesses a number of interrelationships with the civil economy – the government might, for example, place weapons production contracts with private manufacturing firms and soldiers might be expected to spend their wages in civil markets. Secondly, expenditure on the military sector, in common with most public spending, is inherently inflationary owing to the fact that a proportion of the resources taxed to pay for it would have been saved from income or profits and therefore removed from circulation. Thirdly, and most significantly, the military sector is the one major area of a modern capitalist economy which is under the direct control of the central government. Economic expansion can therefore be effected immediately by, say, the ordering of a new weapons system; in contrast, indirect policies such as marginal tax changes would take a much longer period to produce noticeable multiplier effects. Such control is also useful in the possible event of excessive expansion of the economy as weapons systems can be immediately cancelled or contracted to help deflate the system.

Once this regulation system has become established, several groups of people will find it economically advantageous to maintain it in existence. These groups will include senior soldiers, the owners and managers of private industries with which the government places defence contracts, and also politicians whose careers are tied to the defence sector. Together, these groups clearly wield considerable economic and political power. In sum, therefore, these four propositions suggest the maintenance of a strong commitment to military expenditure in capitalist countries for purely economic reasons.

Although C. Wright Mills first put forward his ideas relating to a coincidence of interests between the military elite and other powerful political and economic classes in 1956 (in *The Power Elite*), we have seen few attempts to justify the theory from an empirical point of view; until recently, most contributions have been in the form of elaborations or extensions of the basic model outlined above. In the past few years, however, several important studies have been undertaken, the results of which are, as is often the case in social science, somewhat contradictory!

Rosen (1973) presents us with a compilation of material in which all aspects of the military-industrial complex are subjected to empirical scrutiny. The work takes account of a considerable quantity of data and explores the degree to which the military and industrial sectors are linked (as well as the nature of this linkage), the methods of weapons procurement and the relationships between defence and politics. Although most of the evidence is drawn from the experience of the

USA, it is believed that the Soviet Union could also possess a form of military-industrial complex, with the state factory managers occupying a similar role to the capitalist factory owners. Given such a diversity of areas of study, unified conclusions are difficult to draw, although Rosen succeeds in summarising the discussion as follows:

> The US and the Soviet Union have developed extensive industrial sectors orientated to military orders for their output. A byproduct of this development is the creation of a class of individuals whose interests are served by defence spending. The careers of related managers and (on the US side) the profits of owners and shareholders are tied to high levels of military preparation. . . These industries are in critical sectors of the economy. On the US side, they include the largest industrial corporations and the crucial capital goods industry. . . On both sides, the most powerful interests in the economy are substantially tied to continued high levels of military production. . . However, neither economy *needs* military spending in the sense that aggregate wealth is dependent on manufacture for defence. The majority of US corporations derive only the smaller part of their sales from military contracts, and defence profits are *not* a disproportionate share of corporate earnings (i.e. profits are not higher in defence). (p. 23)

In a further study of the post-war US economy, Cypher (1974) reaches a similar conclusion, although he is prepared to assert it much more strongly. Concentrating particularly on the use of military expenditure to control the macroeconomy, he concludes that:

> Throughout the postwar era military expenditures have been the major instrument of capitalist planning. Military expenditures have been the largest single controllable item in the arsenal of planning devices which the 'State' has at its disposal. Through the multiplier effect roughly 25 per cent of the GNP in any given postwar year has been (directly or indirectly) generated by military expenditures. The partial generation of postwar 'prosperity' through the creation of roughly $2 trillion of military waste is certainly one of the most glaring postwar capitalist contradictions. (p. 14)

In contrast to the single-nation time-series studies, Smith (1977) has analysed the military-industrial complex theory by means of a cross-section. Taking data for fifteen capitalist DCs, he argues that, if the theory is correct, nations with higher per capita incomes should require high levels of military spending to reabsorb the economic surplus (or to avoid 'underconsumption'). Such a hypothesis is not borne out in practice. Secondly, he argues that the theory predicts low unemployment levels for nations which employ high levels of defence expenditure and, again, there exists little empirical support for such a belief.

The validity of the 'complex' theory as an explanation of trends in capitalist defence expenditures therefore remains unproven. However, it is probably safe to accept Rosen's general conclusions relating to expenditures in the USA and the USSR, as it is only these nations which fully meet the requirements of the military-industrial complex theory. Other nations have yet to develop a sufficiently large defence sector, a sizeable economic surplus and military-industrial linkages; indeed, Smith's data could be taken as evidence for this possibility.

This being so, the 'complex' theory will provide little direct assistance in understanding expenditure trends in the Third World, where the economic surplus is non-existent and fiscal systems remain relatively unsophisticated. Two associated issues are, however, of the utmost importance in this context. The first is the possibility of a correlation between defence spending and economic growth, and this will be dealt with in the next chapter; the second issue concerns us now.

Vested interests.   The 'complex' theory suggested that it was possible for interest groups to support high levels of defence spending owing to the economic advantages thereby secured. One obvious such group is the military itself, which generally possesses the monopoly of power in a nation and therefore represents the ultimate mundane authority. Indeed, a number of LDCs, characterised by imperfect socialisation and the inadequate establishment of civilian rule, have experienced increased in expenditure prompted by pressure from the military itself.

Uganda is a case in point, as Lofchie (1972) has shown. Concerning himself primarily with Amin's seizure of power in 1971, he finds it necessary to go back to 1964 and the East African army mutinies in order to fully understand the nature of the coup d'état. The ways in which the three nations dealt with their respective problems throws considerable light upon subsequent events. Kenya's policy was to remove the ringleaders and steps were taken to enhance the professional standing of the armed forces along conventional DC lines; after 1964 there was a greater tendency to educate indigenous officers at foreign military academies. In contrast to this Kenyan policy, Tanzania eliminated the mutineers and began a policy of military integration into the corpus of civil society.

In the Ugandan case, however, the civilian government took the mutiny as an omen of a potential coup and adopted the policy of acceding to the military's demands. There was a substantial resource reallocation in favour of the army – the 1969 UN *Statistical Yearbook* records that the defence budget rose from £0.50m in 1963 (having remained virtually constant since 1960) to £1.45m in 1964, to £2.47m in 1965, reaching £5.27m by 1968. 'Africanisation' of the officer corps was accelerated and large pay-rises were granted, especially to the non-commissioned ranks who came to receive over twice the incomes of their counterparts in the other East African nations. These factors, coupled with the other obvious benefits of military life in the LDCs, such as the cheapness of subsistence and the possibilities of profiteering amongst the officers, led to the establishment of a marked division between the military and the rest of the population – mainly peasant farmers – and resulted in the self-recognition of the military as a coherent class. The logical conclusion of Obote's 'move to the left' in 1967, which threatened the interests of this class, was the use of force in the maintenance of the preferential position, a conclusion which resulted in the military takeover.

Few examples of the power of the military in raising the defence allocation exist which are as clear-cut as in the Ugandan case. The thesis remains plausible however, and we must conclude that the military itself, by virtue of its power, possesses the potential strength and ability to cause defence expenditures to rise disproportionately.

National Identity.   The military establishments of the Third World nations may also take on an ideological function. The creation of an armed force is one of the primary manifestations of the independence of a new nation.

> An effective army, and eventually a navy and air force, may be one way of creating a national image of a 'modern' state.
>
> (Gutteridge, 1965, p. 58)

Such an image might be desirable, for example, to attract foreign capital into the country concerned. It is also via the medium of national service that doctrines and social attitudes can most easily be disseminated, which accounts for the popularity of short-term conscription amongst the newer states. It would seem probable that a part of Africa's defence growth can be explained in terms of this ideological facet of the military. However, the success of such a venture naturally depends upon the degree of control exercised over the military by the central government – the potential frailty of such control has been demonstrated by the occurrence of popularly-supported military coups, such as that in Ghana in 1966. This ideological function of the military is most important in the Third World context, and it receives more attention at a later stage.

Imperialism. Our final reason for expenditure growth is largely restricted to DCs and relates to the need to retain control of an empire. Given the political history of the globe since 1945, such empires are no longer common, and the only recent example of a major imperial power is Portugal.

Up until the mid-1970s, Portugal was one of the few European states which formally possessed colonies, namely, the three African territories of Angola, Mozambique and Portuguese Guinea. Even when the majority of African nations were granted their independence in the late 1950s and early 1960s, Portugal held firm to its empire and gave little evidence of ever wishing to relinquish its hold.

The liberation of Africa produced a demonstration effect upon the inhabitants of the Portuguese empire and, from this time, we observed the emergence of armed struggle against Portuguese domination. The reaction by Portugal was also in terms of increased military activity. Whilst, during the 1950s, the Portuguese defence budget rose at an average DC rate of a few percentage points each year, the growing strength of the colonial liberation movements (such as the MPLA in Angola and FRELIMO in Mozambique) necessitated an expenditure escalation. Between 1960 and 1974 (the year of the Portuguese coup and the year preceding the independence of Angola and Mozambique), the Portuguese annual defence budget *tripled* – in contrast, the NATO total increased by 25 per cent over the period, whilst the UK budget grew by 14 per cent.[18] In 1972, the Portuguese Army was composed of 180,000 men, 140,000 of which were stationed in one of the three African colonies.[19] Indeed, by 1974, Portugal was devoting a more substantial share of national income to defence than any other European country, and it also possessed the highest rate of defence expenditure growth in that region.

Related to imperialism is the more prevalent form of international economic influence, namely, neo-colonialism. The degree of control over the LDC which might be extended by a neo-colonialist DC will vary from case to case. At the simplest level, the LDC might simply provide a strategic site for a military base, or alternatively, military aid might be provided by the DC. In the most extreme form, a whole range of political, economic and military ties may be established, relating to defence agreements, trade, industrial production and so forth.

The pattern of neo-colonialism is best illustrated by the USA experience. Baran and Sweezy (1968) argue that, in the past one hundred years, America has developed its own 'empire' of effective control, based upon infiltration into industrial ownership, direct economic aid to sympathetic regimes, and also military assistance to such regimes which, of course, implies a causal factor in the growth in US military spending. They cite an impressive list of thirty-three countries, excluding the USA itself, where such neo-colonialism occurs.[20] In terms of defence assistance the sums involved are substantial, as we shall see in Chapter 4.

Clearly, the military costs of imperialism and, of more contemporary significance, of neo-colonialism are borne primarily by the DCs. It was from their number, after all, that the major imperialist powers first emerged – France, Holland, Portugal, the UK – whilst the present role of the neo-colonialists has largely been taken on by the two main 'superpowers' – the USA and USSR. This is not to say, however, that the transfer of military resources is one-way; nor is it true that the involved LDCs find their role in the scheme of things costless. Indeed, LDCs could find that their military commitments are expanded under a neo-colonialist regime, for two major reasons. First, they might well be obliged to develop their own defence facilities in order to complement the military assistance provided by the DC in question. Secondly, LDCs under a neo-colonialist regime are frequently characterised by social tensions and civil strife, precipitated by popular opposition to the neo-colonialist power – the Latin American countries are cases in point. This being so, increased military effort, which generally implies increased military expenditure, will be necessary for counter-insurgency purposes. We might also add that we cannot exclude the possibility that rapid socio-economic development attained by certain LDCs could lead these countries into imperialist ventures of their own, necessitating corresponding rises in military spending on the parts of all concerned.

DEFENCE AND PUBLIC EXPENDITURES

Despite differences in ideology, the economic functions of government differ little from country to country. In the majority of the world's economies, governments are empowered to raise revenue by means of forms of taxation and are further required to allocate these resources to a variety of sectors. Although it seems generally agreed that, in quantitative terms, education, public health and defence are to be the three major recipients of public funds, countries naturally vary when it comes to an assessment of the relative importance of one sector *vis-à-vis* another. In addition, each nation will possess its own list of priorities for sectoral expansion. This can be seen quite clearly from Table 2.4.

TABLE 2.4 Allocation of Public Expenditure By Region, 1970, expressed in $US per capita; growth rates expressed as average annual percentage rates for the period 1961–70

	Defence		Education		Health	
	Amount	Growth	Amount	Growth	Amount	Growth
North America	352	⎫	270	⎫	131	⎫
Western Europe		⎬ 2·6		⎬ 8·0		⎬ 6·2
and WTO	136	⎭	108	⎭	60	⎭
Middle East	44	⎫	16	⎫	5	⎫
South Asia	3		2		1	
Far East	12	⎬ 8·0	12	⎬ 7·5	1	⎬ 2·0
Africa	4		8		3	
Latin America	10	⎭	15	⎭	5	⎭
WORLD	57		46		22	

Source: USACDA (1972), Table III, p. 14, and Chart III, p. 4.

These data indicate that defence is the single most important item in average world public expenditure; indeed, it is the single most significant item in all regions except Africa and Latin America. In cases such as the Middle East, this is only to be expected in view of the conflicts in this region.

Possibly the more alarming statistics are those relating to growth rates. In the DC case, the relative rates tell us that defence expenditure has a declining share of overall public expenditure, whilst the converse is true for the DCs – here, defence is a significant item in the budget, and its relative importance is growing.

Over the past 15–20 years, there have appeared a considerable number of empirical investigations – Sahni (1972) cites over two dozen – which attempt to determine patterns of allocation both between the public and private sectors and within the public sector itself. As we have seen, defence spending is a major component of most economies' public sectors and we should naturally anticipate some military contribution to the determined relationships. Despite the fact that all of the studies are concerned with the public sector and its linkages with the wider economy, we can classify them into two types on the basis of approach. These types may be termed (i) cross-section, (ii) time-series, and we now review examples of each.

Cross-section.   Although a number of the early economists suspected the existence of a relationship between the size of the public sector and the level of economic development, the first theoretical statement was made by Adolf Wagner in the late nineteenth century, and the concept has now become known as 'Wagner's Law'. Wagner argued that public expenditure could be divided into two categories, security and welfare, and that security expenditure was bound to increase with the growth of the 'progressive' state as armies became larger and more capital-intensive. In addition, further intra-state conflict between individuals was generated by industrialisation, necessitating increased police control. In a similar manner, welfare expenditures would also increase with the level of economic development as the state gradually took on many of the private sectors' former responsibilities, such as education and public health, which Wagner (in common with many contemporary governments) believed it could provide more effectively.

Naturally, this 'Law' of expanding state activity has been severely criticised by commentators who argue, for example, that it is wrong to regard the development process as a unique, linear trend, common to all nations.[21] However, taking the 'Law' at face value and applying it to the present subject-matter, we should anticipate a positive correlation between the level of economic development (measured by, for example, per capita income) and the relative size of the defence sector (that is, the defence burden, or defence expenditure as a proportion of national income).

A number of studies have been undertaken in this area. Martin and Lewis (1956) did, for example, conclude that richer countries possessed higher burdens, although their sample of six DCs and ten LDCs is really too small to make any meaningful inferences.

In a more ambitious project, Lotz (1970) investigated several components of public expenditure, of which defence was one. A factor analysis of 37 LDCs (using mid-1960s cross-section data) resulted in

Lotz's conclusion that defence spending was *not* closely related to the particular stage of economic development.

In order to isolate the determinants of the defence burden (D/Y), Lotz performed a regression analysis on the data and included, as independent variables, GNP per head (Y/P), mineral and oil exports (MX) which were a proxy for natural resource endowments, the proportion of the population which was urbanised (U) and the total government budget as a share of income (B/Y). The result was as follows:[22]

$$D/Y = 0.262 - 0.006 \ Y/P + 0.020 \ MX + 0.048 \ U + 0.081 \ B/Y$$
$$\qquad\qquad (-3.51) \qquad (1.80) \qquad\quad (2.64) \qquad (2.19)$$
$$R^2 = 0.366$$

The final coefficient is exactly in line with the predictions of Wagner's Law; the total budget and the defence budget appear to be positively associated. Furthermore, if we take urbanisation as a 'rough-and-ready' proxy for the level of economic development, the predicted result is again confirmed. A slightly less statistically sound relationship is observed between defence and natural resource endowments, although we should expect a good 'fit' for theoretical reasons – nations with abundant resources can afford to spend on defence, and they will also be anxious to protect their wealth from external aggression or from internal secessionist movements. The Biafra/Nigeria conflict is an example of the latter point.

In spite of these significant results, the anticipated relationship between defence and income does not appear; rather the relationship is inverse, and this result is confirmed by the value of the correlation coefficient between D/Y and Y/P, estimated at -0.16. Lotz explains this by the hypothesis that there exists a certain minimum size for a military establishment, determined by technical factors, which implies a fixed expenditure level irrespective of the size of national income. Smaller, poorer nations have therefore been obliged to spend more than their 'fair share' on defence owing to their fears of the mobilisation of other, more affluent states.

Using the IISS data from Table 2.3, we may examine some similar relationships for current data. As information for some countries was unavailable, a number of the 91 nations represented were excluded, as were the USA and USSR 'superpowers', in the belief that their individually enormous military expenditures would introduce a bias into the results. This selection provides us with a sample of 83 nations – 30 DCs and 53 LDCs – and the results of a correlation analysis appear in Table 2.5.

TABLE 2.5   Correlation Coefficients

Variables	Full Sample	DCs only	LDCs only
Defence expenditure and GNP	0·899	0·831	0·461
Defence burden and per capita GNP	−0·149	−0·430	0·240

Our first set of correlations suggest that the richer the nation then the more resources it devotes to defence, both being expressed in absolute terms. This relationship is particularly strong for the DCs and is to be expected on an intuitive level – the richer the nation, the more the economy can afford to divert resources away from civil production. The slightly-weaker LDC relationship is also consistent with the above, but might also lend support to the Lotz thesis, that a number of the poorer nations are obliged to 'overspend' for strategic reasons.

As far as the defence burden is concerned, the DC sample displays quite a strong negative correlation – high burdens are associated with lower, rather than higher, incomes. This apparent reversal of that which was predicted can be explained by considering the nations included in the DC sample.

First, many of the medium-to-high income nations are members of alliances and this factor is significant. As defence exhibits almost pure public goods properties (i.e. if any amount is provided to one member of a group then it is provided equally to all), defensive alliances are regarded as being efficient in that partners can agree on the provision of the appropriate amount of defence which each may consume, and they may then share the costs between themselves. However, once an alliance has been established, it will be in the interests of members to 'free-ride' i.e. to contribute as small a share of the resources as possible, in the hope that a more risk-averse or wealthy partner will subsidise them. This is certainly the case in NATO and WTO, where most of the medium-income nations contribute less than the average burden of 5 per cent and 11 per cent respectively; they are, in fact, heavily subsidised by the extra expenditure undertaken by the USA and USSR (not included in the sample), whose defence burdens exceed the alliances' averages and whose individual strategies dictate that defence escalation must continue.

Secondly, several high-income nations, such as Switzerland, Sweden and Japan, remain outside the defensive alliances and have not become involved in the arms race which has, to some extent, been forced upon NATO and WTO by the superpowers. The requirements of the alliances which oblige most NATO and WTO members to attempt to 'follow the leaders' mean that the average defence burden in the allied nations is about twice that of the unaligned countries (3.5 per cent compared to 1.7 per cent).

Thirdly, several of the low-income DCs possess high defence burdens for a variety of reasons. Whilst for some, such as Greece and Turkey, this is a result of internal turmoil, others have found it necessary to spend on defence owing to their exclusion from alliances – Albania, for example, left WTO in 1968 and now prefers to defend itself in isolation. Both it and Yugoslavia find themselves in a strategically dangerous position on the interface between the 'First' and 'Second' worlds. In such cases, isolationism has posed security problems and necessitated correspondingly high levels of defence provision.

Returning to the IISS sample of LDCs, we detect here the positive association as originally predicted by Wagner's Law. Given such conflicting evidence, we are therefore obliged to ask – how useful are such cross-section studies? Whilst some of the conclusions are quite valuable, such as those of Lotz regarding the problems of the smaller nations, it must be admitted that the central arguments of Wagner's Law are unlikely to provide a useful framework for analysis of the defence or general public sectors. The central problem of cross-section studies is the lack of any historical dimension. Whilst it might certainly be true that there exist certain tendencies towards public sector expansion with development, each country will be following its own particular path through time, encountering its own peculiar economic, political and strategic problems. Countries at a similar stage of development (even assuming that this can be defined) might therefore possess completely different sizes of public sector and defence budgets. Examples from our data are Israel and New Zealand, both with per capita incomes of around $3,500 but with defence burdens of 33.9 per cent and 1.7 per cent respectively. Again, Afghanistan and Bangladesh are, in many ways, similar countries (including an almost identical level of per capita income), yet the former's defence burden is nearly four times that of the latter.

An additional problem with cross-section studies is their sensitivity to the basic data. Even assuming the latter to be accurate and commensurable, the number of observations in the sample, and the time-period selected, are clearly crucial. A cross-section of the LDCs today, for example, would yield different results from a 1958 study owing to such factors as the disproportionate rise in the defence budgets of the nations of the Middle East and Africa.

Time-series. The time-series approach, which examines changes in the size and composition of the public sector of one particular nation over a period of time, was developed largely as a reaction to the limitations of cross-section methods. Two of the earliest analysts of the UK experience – Peacock and Wiseman (1961) – explain their approach as follows:

> Both the secular character and the 'historical inevitability' of Wagner's Law make difficulties for the development of ideas about government expenditure. . . We must seek, not universal secular laws, but a way of looking at year-to-year changes in government spending that will not only illuminate the British statistics. . ., but also give us an approach to the subject that might be equally fruitful in studying other countries or periods. . . (p. 24–5)

However, in spite of the explicit rejection of the universalism of the cross-section approach, Peacock and Wiseman came to the conclusion that defence expenditure was still a major determinant of the growth of the public sector, and the basic argument runs as follows.

Put very crudely, the size of the public sector is determined by how much the citizens of the country are prepared to pay in the form of taxation. Peacock and Wiseman argue that, under normal circumstances and when societies are not subjected to 'unusual pressures', popular attitudes towards the tolerable burden of taxation are stable over time, implying that public expenditure grows roughly in line with national output. However, abnormal circumstances, such as the occurrence of major wars, dictate that taxation must be increased to finance military activity, and this necessity, it is argued, will be rationalised and accepted by the taxpayers who clearly have an interest in self-protection. However, the tolerable tax burden will be subsequently redefined at the new level, once normal circumstances have been restored. This sequential process accordingly implies a progressive increase in the proportion of national output which is allocated to the public sector.

People will accept, in times of crisis, methods of raising revenue formerly thought intolerable, and the acceptance of the new tax levels remains when the disturbance has disappeared. (op. cit. p. xxiv)

The UK economy during the twentieth century provided the evidence for this theory – public revenue can be represented as an increasing 'step-function' or 'displacement' of income over time, the 'steps' coinciding with periods of national disturbance, in particular the two major wars. With the passing of the crisis, the military budget tended to contract and the additional resources were expended on other government programmes, such as health and education.

A direct parallel to the Peacock/Wiseman analysis of the UK is the experience of the USA during the Korean crisis and the rearmament boom of the early 1950s. An increase in defence spending was budgeted for 1950 and was mainly financed by increased taxation on personal incomes and corporation profits. The major defence growth began during 1951, when military expenditure was estimated to rise from $20,994m to $41,421m before the end of the fiscal year 1952. By way of contrast, the total for all other government functions was estimated to rise from $15,768m to $16,815m during the same period; in percentage terms, these figures represent an annual growth rate of 97 per cent and 7 per cent respectively.

The primary aim of the Administration's tax policy in 1951 was to secure a prompt enactment of tax increases large enough to eliminate the deficit that was in prospect for fiscal 1952 if defence expenditures rose as expected and tax rates were not raised. (Holmans, 1961, p. 156)

Taxation revenue was therefore again raised from the same sources as before, with the addition of substantial rises in excise duties.

The scale of rearmament at this time was considerable; defence expenditure rose from 5.8 per cent of GNP in 1949 to 14.5 per cent in 1952. Although all of the nations which had participated in the Second World War expanded their defence sectors simultaneously, the growth in the USA was the largest and the most rapid. Furthermore, it was financed almost exclusively by taxation – between 1949 and 1952, taxation receipts rose from 23.8 per cent to 28.4 per cent of GNP.

At the end of the war in 1945, attempts had been made to lower the level of taxation entailed by the conflict. By 1949, taxation was running at around 19–20 per cent of GNP. After the rearmament period, tax reductions also occurred, but during the 1950s the level never fell below 20 per cent; stabilisation finally occurred at a little above this figure. By 1970, the federal tax level had reached 22 per cent of GNP.[23] This time-trend seems to indicate a 'step' of the Peacock/Wiseman type and provides supporting evidence for the displacement theory.

The displacement hypothesis is difficult to test in the Third World context, however, owing to its data requirements – few LDCs possess sufficiently accurate or lengthy time-series to permit analysis, and many which do have been involved in perennial conflicts. In theory, however, we should expect such an effect to be present. In many cases in the Third World, the government sees itself as the most effective allocater of resources and, when it finds extra funds in its hands as a result of a 'step' in the tolerable tax burden, it will often use them for poverty relief, infrastructural development and other investment programs, just as in the DC case. To take the example of Ghana, we find that defence expenditure was cut by 13 per cent between 1969 and 1972, having previously been raised as a result of the 1966 coup and the resultant unrest. Taxation receipts, however, were increased by 69 per cent. These additional resources were channelled into other areas of the public sector, notably education (whose allocation rose by 43 per cent) and public health (whose allocation rose by 26 per cent) and this pattern is followed by other LDCs which have experienced rapid rises and falls in defence spending – for example, India, Nigeria and Guatemala.[24]

Before concluding our review of the time-series approach, it is instructive to examine its relationship with the cross-section studies, for such a relationship does exist and, as such, could throw some light on to why the latter studies periodically produce good results. If we accept that, by and large, defence is the only commodity which taxpayers will willingly subsidise under the threat of annihilation, we arrive at defence as the 'prime mover' of the total public budget. In a time of crisis, defence spending expands and therefore public expenditure expands; when the crisis is over, the military budget gradually contracts and the resources are diverted to other ends such as welfare facilities. Given that nations tend to undergo a process of economic development over time (i.e. development and time are collinear) it is clear that the implications of the time-series approach satisfy the predictions of Wagner's Law, even if the causation is different.

What can be concluded from such empirical studies of defence and public expenditure? First, it seems unlikely that any 'universal, secular laws' exist to change the nature of the public sector as economic development progresses. Secondly, it is reasonable to assert that defence spending must be a major determinant of the behaviour of any one public sector, in view of its magnitude, with the result that any changes in military spending must influence the total. Thirdly, the view that the tolerable tax burden shifts with military spending appears to be borne out in practice for major changes in taxation levels such as were required in European countries during the 1939–45 period. With respect to *minor* changes in the tax burden, however, the evidence is much less clear, and we should be quite willing to accept that taxpayers would agree to marginal increases in the burden in return for social welfare benefits such as education and health – indeed, Peacock and Wiseman (1961) provide substantive evidence for this in the British case.

The third point gives us two complementary propositions of some significance – (i) defence expenditure necessitated by a crisis can cause increasing welfare expenditure when the crisis recedes and the defence budget becomes progressively smaller in a larger total, and (ii) welfare budgets might marginally expand of their own volition owing to conscious public policy and the acceptance thereof by the political process.

These propositions lead us to the important conclusion that, as far as public expenditure is concerned, defence and social welfare expenditures need not be substitutes. In the first case, the former can actually bring about the latter whilst, in the second, the latter expands independently. We should therefore be quite prepared to discover a positive correlation between welfare and defence budgets and a number of studies have, in fact, obtained this. Lotz (1970) derived a correlation coefficient of 0.20 between these two variables for his 37 LDCs, whilst Kennedy (1974), examining a wider LDC sample and using UN public finance data, concluded that:

> The evidence does not suggest that high defence budgets are necessarily at the expense of welfare budgets... The evidence suggests that governments have increased expenditures on all items rather than re-allocate between them. (pp. 72 and 74)

In one sense, of course, military expenditure *is* a substitute for welfare and other civil spending in that the expenditure on defence *could* potentially have been used in other ways. Whilst the 'dove' element of a population might regard any level of military expenditure as a total waste of valuable resources, the vast majority of national governments appear to believe that some amount of defence spending is necessary for the reasons previously discussed. The question therefore becomes, not whether to spend on defence at all, but, rather, *how much* to spend to achieve the desired ends. Clearly, the answer to this will involve an assessment of the appropriate objectives of defence spending and, as we shall see in the next chapter, an evaluation of the economic costs and benefits of the defence budget.

3 Defence and the Economy

The purpose of this chapter is to provide an evaluation of the actual costs of defence spending in terms of the utilisation of resources. We shall be mainly concerned with the internal aspects of defence, that is, the repercussions of *domestic* military spending upon the *domestic* economy. This emphasis will be reversed in the following chapter, however, which examines the 'external' aspects, those involving *international* defence expenditures.

The opportunity costs of defence are not so clear-cut that we may simply infer that expenditure on defence entails a net withdrawal of the corresponding amount of resources from economic circulation. This is because defence expenditure itself produces both beneficial and detrimental effects upon the civil economy. Before examining defence costs, it is therefore necessary to analyse certain areas of activity where the military and the civil economy impinge upon one another.

DEFENCE INDUSTRIES

Amongst the nations of the developed world, heavy investment in the defence sector and, in particular, in those industries producing military requirements, has been partially justified in terms of the existence of 'spin-off'. The argument revolves around the possibility of the transfer of technology from 'military' to 'civil' industry. Expenditure on military research and development, it is said, might produce new knowledge, techniques and materials which may have direct civilian applications, and the use of this new technology would clearly increase the economy's productive potential.

The industrial experiences of the United Kingdom and the United States of America provide many examples which support the belief in the existence of spin-off. During the nineteenth century, small-arms manufacture entailed the standardisation of components and production-line systems, both of whose principles were readily applicable, and were indeed essential, to the machine-tool industry. New steel alloys were developed to cater for the requirements of heavier armaments and these found alternative applications in civil engineering. More recently, the US aero-space programmes have provided spin-offs by advancing technology in a number of fields, from medicine to micro-electronics, from computers to cooking utensils.[1]

Because the exploitation of spin-off presupposes the existence of some form of coherent industrial structure in both civil and military industry, the concept is inapplicable in its present form to the majority of LDCs. As we shall see, these nations have placed great reliance on purchases of weaponry from NATO and Warsaw Pact countries to build up their own armed forces – virtually all of the major weapons in Africa, for example, have been obtained from these two blocs. So far, few completely successful attempts have been made in creating truly indigenous arms industries and so the likelihood of spin-off hardly arises, particularly when one comes to consider the embryonic nature of overall LDC industrialisation.

At the present time, about two dozen LDCs are engaged in some form of domestic production of major weapons, although a much greater number currently produce relatively simple and inexpensive items such as small arms and ammunition.[2] The evolution of military production has been fairly common to all these Third World nations. In the first instance, expertise was gained by the servicing and maintenance of imported hardware, leading to the licensed or sponsored production of similar equipment within the LDC itself. Completely indigenous production – from the design to the manufacturing stage – has finally become feasible in a number of cases.

All types of major weapons are currently produced in the Third World, although the form of production does vary from weapon to weapon. Most of the arms-producing LDCs are now able to equip their navies with at least some completely indigenous warships, whereas most of such countries' air forces still tend to be made up of DC aeroplanes produced under licence in the LDC concerned. Over the past few years, the Third World has made rapid strides towards indigenous production in this area, as it has in the field of guided missiles – Argentina, Brazil, China and India are presently flying aircraft and missiles of completely indigenous manufacture.

The evolution of defence industries in India over the past twenty years provides an interesting example of the interrelationships between defence expenditure and development, in terms of industrialisation. In India, spin-off has gone further than the simple transfer of technology, although this aspect certainly plays a part. By virtue of military production, certain branches of civil industry have been made viable and new industrial sectors have evolved in parallel with military industry.[3]

Ordnance factories had been established in India under the British regime, although it was not until 1945 that directives were issued to determine their future role. The range of industrial activities was deliberately widened so that military industry could be successfully integrated into the civil economy at all levels. How did this work in practice?

In 1960, the Marazon Docks complex and the Garden Reach Workshops, formerly under British ownership, were offered for sale and were purchased by the Department of Defence Production. Although primarily intended for the construction of the Indian Navy's warships, the docks soon had orders for two large liners and found themselves in great demand for the maintenance and repairing of both military and civil shipping. In addition, many small-scale projects were undertaken, such as the construction of barges and tugs, and the resulting revenues allowed the workshops to diversify and to establish new units for the manufacture of diesel engines, compressors, cranes and pumps.

A similar pattern is displayed by aircraft manufacture. The Hindustan Aircraft Company was taken over by the Ministry of Defence in 1943 for aircraft construction but, by 1959, it had become apparent that some scope existed for the production of civil aircraft. The Indian government had originally hoped for self-sufficiency in the manufacture of aeroplanes within twenty years, but it now seems that such an achievement is unlikely until the 1980s. Production commenced with the conversion of war-surplus machines, notably the Douglas C-47s, and developed into the assembly of British aircraft. The efforts of the past decade have been aimed at the manufacture of supersonic fighters, helicopters, light aircraft and transports for civil/military usage. An example of the latter is the HS-748, which was originally designed for use with the armed forces but which was later successfully sold to India's civil airlines.

Amongst the smaller industries, the military's electronics establishments provide many of the armed forces' requirements. They are presently expanding into the civil market with the supply of radio components, transmitters and receivers, as well as navigational aids for shipping. Developments in the computer field are also being planned.

The civil/military linkages in the Indian economy are clearly well-established. Indeed, in some cases, the trend has been reversed; Praga Tools was incorporated into the military sector to provide engineering components, despite the fact that its output remains predominantly concerned with the civil sector – lathes, milling and foundry work.

In theory, such a policy as has been pursued by the Indian government with respect to defence could yield many economic advantages. Possibly the most obvious is that of foreign exchange savings. Shipping and aeroplanes are two of the most expensive defence items and so, via domestic production, valuable funds are liberated for alternative uses. Furthermore, such industry can provide employment and training opportunities for local labour, which will naturally produce a beneficial economic effect.

Equally important is the consideration of capacity utilisation. Large-scale industry, with high unit-cost products, tends to be demand-deficient, especially in low-income countries. It is clear that, individually, neither civilian nor military demand alone could sustain an aircraft or a shipbuilding industry – together, however, they permit continuous production from an established plant. Furthermore, the military (and therefore the government) is able to manipulate its construction requirements as a policy tool, by phasing its demand to coincide with slack periods within the civilian area of the market.

Such composite demand might also be necessary to justify the establishment of new industries. Because of their lack of resources, LDCs are generally only able to promote a new industry either by state financing, or by permitting the introduction of a foreign-owned enterprise. This latter course is frequently considered undesirable, owing to the problems of repatriation of profits and the possibility of political and economic involvement in state affairs. It might therefore be to a country's advantage to consider the establishment of an industry under the auspices of defence, to provide for the nation's weaponry and to economise on foreign exchange. Such a policy would have the important effect of permitting parallel civil production of a similar product with similar benefits.

Military demand of this nature can only be a spur to development in a relatively small sector of the economy, namely that concerned with technology, engineering and transport. Nevertheless, it is just this sector that many LDCs are attempting to encourage, to enable them to follow their development ideals. A role therefore does exist for the military in demand creation and stabilisation. Even so, because of the nature of the demand structure of military industry, it is essential that expenditure on defence industries occurs within the context of a coherent planning framework, to ensure that the required economic linkages exist. An illustration of this is the necessity of having available sufficient quantities of iron and steel and other metals, these being the main components of most military equipment. Should these be unavailable within the country concerned, the establishment of the defence industry will simply entail an increase in raw material imports, thus eliminating any potential benefits. Almost certainly, such importation will be necessary in the short run; steps must therefore be taken to ensure that the burden will not have to continue into the longer term.

In theory therefore, we can easily justify the establishment of defence industries within Third World countries. However, if we examine the Indian situation more closely, we discover that these potential long-term benefits have only been achieved through considerable short-term costs.

In common with most LDCs, India had to face a number of problems in defence industry development. First, there was a general shortage of financial resources, with the result that expenditure on defence necessitated economies elsewhere. Secondly, weapons production required raw materials of a specialist type which were frequently in limited supply – steel, rarer metals, electronic components – and this led to increases in imports. Finally, manufacture of armaments required a particular type of skilled labour which implied that substantial amounts of resources had to be devoted to training.

Initial developments in the Indian military industry were concerned with the licensed production and/or assembly of foreign weaponry in the belief that savings could be made by domestic production. For example, the 1956 construction cost of the HS-748 was originally estimated at $320,000, as compared to an import price of $1m; the current production cost now stands at $1.5m, however. Similarly, the Gnat fighter now has a unit cost of $2.5m, a figure certainly in excess of the import price of a comparative completed aircraft.

Why should it be cheaper to import finished machines from abroad? First, cheap labour forms the major production advantage of the LDCs, but this is of little value in the arms industries, which tend to be capital-intensive, and labour costs therefore represent only a small proportion of the total. Material costs for LDCs tend to be high as (i) locally-produced components often have to be subsidised to encourage indigenous production, (ii) parts imported from DCs are frequently expensive relative to the costs of completed machines, owing to transport costs and to the realisation on the part of DC suppliers that the strong desire of LDCs to assemble their own equipment means that profit margins may safely be increased. LDCs also suffer in that they seldom possess adequate facilities for testing and they are often obliged to transport their completed machines to DCs for this purpose. In addition, in the short run, LDCs will be unable to reap full economies of scale and will suffer from resource starvation in the field of research and development, although one of India's current policies is the rectification of this omission.

If we depart from this standard analysis, however, we are at liberty to question whether the absolute production cost is an adequate reflection of the true opportunity cost because, in terms of community preference, it makes no distinction between foreign and domestic resources. Being more scarce, it seems plausible that the former should be valued more highly. This being so, comparison in terms of foreign exchange reveals a different picture, such that it now becomes profitable for the domestic industry to produce a proportion of Indian requirements, in particular the Gnat and the Mig-21. For example, the foreign exchange cost of production for the Gnat has been estimated at $US110,000 or 55 per cent of the import cost.[4]

The Indian shipbuilding industry has fared much better in terms of pure economics. Profits have been steadily increasing, although a foreign exchange outflow has lately occurred owing to the purchase of naval weaponry, electronics and other equipment. In terms of the plans of the Indian government, however, this industry has not been accorded as high a priority as aircraft manufacture. This fact is a reflection of the realisation that, in strategic terms, conflict is more likely to arise on land and in the air than at sea.

In sum, therefore, it would seem that the establishment of defence industries, such as in India, may prove to be an expensive operation. However, as we have already noted, this has not deterred a number of LDCs from the development of such industry in order to supply at least some of their armies' requirements by indigenous production. Indeed, there are a number of sound reasons for such a policy. Given that a prime concern of the Third World is strategy, the LDCs will be anxious to minimise their dependence upon the established power blocs who currently hold the monopoly of arms sales; nor can they afford to risk the possibility of a shortfall in supply should this be determined by outside circumstances. Furthermore, the purchase of foreign weapons is expensive and, for a country which has attained a fair degree of industrialisation, the economic costs of local production might not be prohibitive, in view of the foreign exchange savings and the boost given to sectoral development by military/civil composite demand. Indeed, a study undertaken by Kennedy (1974) appears to support this view, for he concludes:

> There is no evidence that it [i.e. domestic military production] wastes resources or holds back growth of the manufacturing sector...The... defence sector is associated with and integrated into the metal and engineering sector, and there appears to be some positive association between the expansion of both sectors. (p. 301)

Such generalisations as to the fortunes of the LDCs in aggregate tend to be somewhat dangerous. India's policy is, at present, extremely expensive, but the government appears confident of returns in the form of exchange savings, capital-deepening and industrial multipliers, to say nothing of the strategic benefits. Indeed, now that the industry has established itself, the estimated production costs for new, indigenously-designed weaponry have decreased considerably. Argentina, on the other hand, serves as an example of a situation where progress may be frustrated by the mismanagement of the defence programme. Because of the instability of government during the past two decades, pro-grammes have been subject to a 'stop-go' policy. Inter-service rivalry has also meant that differential weight has been attached to different sectors at different times. For example, during the Peron era, investment in aviation increased enormously, resulting in the development and testing of a number of prototypes of indigenous design. However, after Peron's departure in 1955, this investment all but came to nothing as production was virtually discontinued. The military regime of the early 1970s has managed to balance out inter-service demands and to subject requirements to more judicious planning. Shipbuilding has also been expanded, with the result that Argentina now possesses one of the most advanced industries of this type, in company with Brazil and India.

What is the future of domestic defence production in the nations of the Third World? Its high costs and industrialisation requirements seem to preclude its development in all but the largest of the LDCs. There is every reason to believe, however, that other nations of the Third World will attempt to enlarge their own armaments sectors as soon as they are able to do so, since, in their view, the additional resource commitment is a small price to pay for the potential long-run economic benefits and the value of non-alignment and political security.

REGIONAL MULTIPLIERS

In keeping with any other form of economic structure, a military establishment, be it industry, barracks or base, does not exist or operate in isolation. Feedback between itself and the surrounding economic environment will occur, and a mutual relationship can be established based upon supply and demand. It therefore follows that such a military installation could generate a beneficial multiplier effect, that is, expenditure on a military establishment could stimulate the demand for local products, resulting in the expansion of economic activity. The calculation of regional multipliers is, in itself, a relatively new addition to the techniques of economic statistics; applications are therefore few in number. Needless to say, even less work has been performed with respect to the Third World, especially in relation to military activities. Our analysis must therefore rely upon the adaptation of DC examples to the LDC environment.

Bolton (1966) has presented the most detailed estimation of the relationships between regional growth and defence spending. By subdividing the USA into regions and states, he was able to estimate the contribution of the central government's defence purchases from local industry to the growth of the region. The model developed is a simple regional base model – it predicts local income as a linear function of exogenous income. The theory stood up well to empirical tests – correlation coefficients of around 0.9 for most regions – and the next step was to estimate the quantity of defence income accruing to each region in terms of the value added. Finally, it was possible to deduce the contribution of defence purchases – in other words, income – to regional growth, for the period 1952–62. A wide spread of estimates resulted, ranging from 27 per cent over the decade for one region, to −21 per cent for another, indicating that defence purchases could even have a depressant effect upon the local economy. One particularly significant feature of the results was the following:

> Neither a high degree of dependence upon defence income nor a very rapid growth in defence income will alone contribute to the growth of the region. Both are necessary. (p. 12)

Weiss and Gooding (1968) attempted a micro-study of defence expenditure related to regional growth. They examined a small community in the USA – Portsmouth, New Hampshire – whose economic activity, in relation to trade with the surrounding region, was geared to (i) a military manufacturing installation, (ii) a non-manufacturing defence base, (iii) a number of civilian industries. Their chosen region was small and closed, so that major second-round import leakages could be neglected. The model employed was similar to that used by Bolton, but it was made a little more sophisticated by the introduction of time-lags into the variables.

As might be expected, the non-manufacturing military base gave rise to the lowest employment multiplier (1.4) owing to the fact that its main purchases, such as equipment and provisions, were made in national, government-directed markets. Similarly much of the income generated by the base was spent within its own confines, as it provided a large proportion of its community's social amenities. This finding is reinforced by other studies of military bases, which Weiss and Gooding cite; these studies conclude that around 40 per cent of payrolls are spent directly within the base itself.

Private industry produced an understandably higher multiplier (1.8) and the manufacturing installation came out with a median value (1.6). The difference in multipliers between these two types of industry may be ascribed to the facts that (i) the installation – a shipyard – required specialist inputs, obtained from national rather than local markets, (ii) a proportion of the yard's labour force lived outside the Portsmouth region and would therefore be likely to spend some of the income elsewhere, (iii) the yard's labour force was highly paid, compared to the region's manufacturing industry, and this might have produced a different consumption pattern, *vis-à-vis* the rest of the community.

These studies throw further light on to the discussion of defence spending as a fiscal agent, a debate which we met in the previous chapter. We observe that both of the theories contain some element of truth. Defence investment does create a multiplier effect, certainly in excess of the deflationary result of public saving. Conversely, as Baran and Sweezy argued, the inflationary effect is less than that obtained from investment in civilian manufacturing. Such a conclusion not only resolves the apparent conflict of the two ideas, but it also suggests that the fiscal role of military spending can yield a finer adjustment than was first supposed, by judicious allocation between military and civilian investments.

How useful are these studies in helping us to understand the problems of the LDCs? At least one of Bolton's conclusions ought to be relevant. He was especially interested in the potential policy tool of tendering defence contracts to those regions where a labour surplus existed. As early as 1951, the US Secretary for Defence appreciated the possibility of such an operation, but it would appear that little has come of the idea. The main problems are the lack of capital capacity and the nature of the labour force, unskilled in the type of work required. These regions clearly have much in common with the LDCs and Bolton's policy conclusion would be equally justified in this latter case. This conclusion is that the subsidisation of capital and training would be economically legitimate in order to develop local defence industries in these regions, but only if alternative forms of industrial production prove to be uneconomic. Third World countries seem to be in more urgent need of general industrialisation than of specifically military industry, and they would therefore be better advised to concentrate on the development of the former. However, given the possibilities of spin-off and the political priorities attached to defence industries, military investment could be considered, especially in the light of what follows.

The Weiss and Gooding model approximates well to a major city within an LDC. If the three types of output specified are to be produced at all, they will be produced within the confines of a substantial conurbation. Moreover, the system would be closed and small as in the Portsmouth case, although this would now be due to the excessive polarisation of economic activity which exists in the LDCs. Some of the provisions of the model do not, however, hold true in the case of a Third World country: Industrial purchases, for example, will most likely come from within the region owing to the small number of alternative markets, although the purchase of consumption goods from abroad could cause additional expense. Demand and supply of the two types of military establishments could therefore be integrated and this would serve to enhance the multiplier effects. In the main, labour would be resident within the region and could be expected to spend its income there, again because of the lack of alternative centres. Coupled with the fact that incomes of government workers are likely to be higher than those of a private industrial work force, we could reasonably expect the multipliers to be higher than in the case of Portsmouth.

Our analysis suggests that, for countries such as India, military industries could generate valuable multipliers within the local economy. However, in the case of the majority of LDCs, where a base is isolated from its sources of supply and where no manufacturing occurs, the resultant multiplier effects are likely to be low. It should be borne in mind, nevertheless, that LDC bases tend to be less sophisticated than their DC counterparts, and it therefore seems probable that a more intimate relationship would be established between the base and the immediate environment, in terms of services, provision of supplies and so on.

In sum, it would appear that defence spending can generate some degree of regional multiplication and would, given an appropriate geographical location, serve as a policy tool in regional development programmes. However, the most pronounced multiplier effects can only be gained at those centres where industrial and infrastructural development is well advanced, and this constraint might run counter to the LDC's desire for depolarisation.

MANPOWER AND EMPLOYMENT

Military expenditure is allocated for the purchase of a number of basic inputs into the defence sector, one of which is labour. Table 3.1, a companion set of data to Table 2.3, presents the most recent estimates for military manpower and related variables. Included in this table are the estimated size of the full-time, professional armed forces, the military participation ratio (i.e. the proportion of the total population employed in the defence sector), the quantity of military expenditure per enlisted man, and the average annual population and manpower growth rates. The results of a correlation analysis of these data are presented in Table 3.2 – again, the 'superpowers' are excluded from the sample, as are those nations for which some of the data are unavailable.

In all cases, there clearly exists a strong positive association between manpower and population, i.e., the nations with the largest populations have the largest armies. In terms of growth, however, we see that it is only in the case of the DCs that military employment has responded positively to changes in population – for the LDCs, the changes in population (generally increases) have not necessarily resulted in changes in the size of the military establishment. Taiwan, Laos, Ghana and Colombia, for example, have all contracted their armed forces in spite of high population growths, whilst Bangladesh, the Philippines and Cuba have all expanded theirs, despite reasonably slow population growth.

Nevertheless, in the next case, aggregate manpower levels do appear to be related to the absolute level of defence spending which, as we know from the previous chapter, is additionally correlated with income.

The correlation between military expenditure and manpower is to be expected in view of the theoretical connection between these two variables. At one level, manpower will be a determinant of expenditure by virtue of its effect on the total wage-bill which, in turn, is a component of overall spending. At another level, the relationship between gross

TABLE 3.1   Military Manpower and Related data for 91 Countries, 1977, in current prices and exchange rates. Growth rates calculated over the past five years. 'n.a.' indicates data are unavailable

Country	Manpower ('000)	Man-power/ Popula-tion (%)	Defence Expen-diture per Man ($'000)	Annual Popula-tion Growth (%)	Annual Man-power Growth (%)
USA	2088	0·96	52·5	0·72	−1·88
Belgium	86	0·86	21·2	0·30	−1·12
Britain	339	0·60	32·1	0·16	−1·58
Canada	80	0·34	45·1	1·18	−0·92
Denmark	35	0·68	31·1	0·35	−3·37
France	502	0·93	23·3	0·84	−0·08
German FR	489	0·77	28·1	1·25	0·73
Greece	200	2·20	5·5	0·54	5·74
Italy	330	0·58	14·1	1·04	−6·27
Luxembourg	0·6	0·18	40·3	0·93	3·25
Netherlands	110	0·79	30·6	0·82	−0·56
Norway	39	0·96	28·7	0·42	2·45
Portugal	59	0·67	7·8	−1·14	−26·73
Turkey	465	1·13	5·7	2·04	0·55
USSR	3675	1·43	34·6	0·73	1·78
Bulgaria	149	1·68	3·6	0·50	−0·58
Czechoslovakia	181	1·21	8·9	0·59	−1·21
German DR	157	0·91	18·4	0·39	4·43
Hungary	103	0·98	5·7	0·24	0·02
Poland	307	0·89	7·9	0·63	2·33
Romania	180	0·83	4·6	0·82	1·44
Albania	45	1·70	3·0	2·51	4·32
Austria	37	0·47	14·3	1·24	−8·00
Eire	15	0·46	10·0	1·63	8·50
Finland	40	0·84	10·7	0·15	0·25
Spain	309	0·85	7·0	1·20	1·34
Sweden	69	0·83	41·3	0·19	−7·37
Switzerland	19	0·28	69·2	0·84	−13·80
Yugoslavia	260	1·20	6·3	0·86	2·02
Australia	70	0·50	40·2	1·85	−1·28
Japan	238	0·21	25·6	1·60	−2·74
New Zealand	12	0·39	16·9	2·00	−0·64
Egypt	345	0·89	12·7	2·16	3·73
Iran	342	0·98	23·1	3·06	12·77
Iraq	188	1·60	8·8	3·86	16·57
Israel	164	4·53	26·0	3·31	11·79

Country	Manpower ('000)	Man-power/ Popula-tion (%)	Defence Expen-diture per Man ($'000)	Annual Popula-tion Growth (%)	Annual Man-power Growth (%)
Jordan	68	2·35	3·0	3·04	51·57
Kuwait	10	0·92	206·0	n.a.	n.a.
Lebanon	18	0·61	3·8	−0·24	4·59
Saudi Arabia	62	0·82	122·4	−2·79	9·68
Syria	228	2·94	4·7	3·42	14·58
N. Yemen	40	0·57	1·5	−0·02	17·51
S. Yemen	21	1·19	2·1	3·50	22·37
Bangladesh	71	0·09	0·7	1·46	41·12
Afghanistan	110	0·55	0·4	2·37	7·00
India	1096	0·18	3·1	1·87	3·69
Pakistan	428	0·58	1·9	3·44	1·58
Sri Lanka	13	0·09	3·6	2·45	1·56
Burma	170	0·52	0·7	2·71	3·28
Taiwan	460	2·67	2·2	3·30	−2·21
Indonesia	247	0·18	5·5	0·63	−6·41
N. Korea	500	3·00	2·0	2·75	1·56
S. Korea	635	1·80	2·8	1·89	0·08
Laos	49	1·39	0·6	2·67	−10·06
Malaysia	64	0·48	8·5	3·78	3·40
Mongolia	30	1·95	4·0	4·24	0·85
Philippines	99	0·22	4·2	3·03	23·40
Singapore	36	1·54	9·4	1·55	14·98
Thailand	211	0·47	3·0	5·27	4·05
China	3950	0·43	6·6	3·70	8·03
Algeria	76	0·42	5·1	3·31	4·73
Libya	29	1·11	7·8	5·05	3·96
Ethiopia	54	0·18	1·9	2·57	4·67
Ghana	18	0·17	7·4	3·43	−1·63
Kenya	8	0·05	4·5	n.a.	n.a.
Morocco	87	0·48	4·0	2·80	11·53
Nigeria	231	0·35	10·4	2·81	10·08
Rhodesia	10	0·14	16·6	3·42	19·39
Senegal	6	0·13	7·9	n.a.	n.a.
Somali	32	0·95	0·8	2·68	16·16
S. Africa	55	0·20	34·5	4·00	21·12
Sudan	52	0·28	2·5	2·34	7·79

Country	Manpower ('000)	Man-power/ Popula-tion (%)	Defence Expen-diture per Man ($'000)	Annual Popula-tion Growth (%)	Annual Man-power Growth (%)
Tanzania	19	0·12	3·8	2·69	12·53
Tunisia	22	0·37	7·0	2·46	−1·93
Uganda	21	0·17	2·3	3·43	13·62
Zaire	33	0·13	2·3	1·90	−9·60
Zambia	9	0·16	36·4	n.a.	n.a.
Argentina	130	0·50	10·9	1·75	−0·96
Bolivia	23	0·38	3·3	2·81	0·79
Brazil	272	0·24	7·6	2·96	6·92
Chile	85	0·77	7·2	4·43	9·10
Colombia	57	0·22	2·5	3·21	−2·76
Cuba	189	1·97	1·5	2·00	14·88
Dominican Rep.	19	0·37	2·3	3·09	4·02
Ecuador	24	0·31	4·8	3·86	1·86
Honduras	14	0·43	1·8	n.a.	n.a.
Mexico	220	0·34	2·5	4·79	2·93
Paraguay	17	0·61	2·1	2·39	3·35
Peru	70	0·41	5·8	3·20	6·70
Uruguay	27	0·86	2·8	1·15	6·48
Venezuela	44	0·35	11·7	2·61	4·08

Source: Derived from IISS (various dates), The Military Balance.

expenditure on factor inputs and one particular input, labour, will be determined by the particular form of military technology appropriate to the country concerned. Generalising from the experience of the Third World and, indeed, from that of the DCs, the evolution of military technology appears to occur via the following stages:

(i) primary reliance upon infantry regiments, equipped with small arms and simple transport facilities,

(ii) expansion of the infantry, to include artillery, tanks, etc.; the development of an air force, and navy if appropriate,

(iii) development of sophisticated conventional weaponry which embodies the most advanced technology, e.g. submarines, missiles with advanced guidance, etc.,

(iv) concentration of efforts on nuclear capabilities.

TABLE 3.2   Correlation Coefficients

Variables	Full Sample	DCs only	LDCs only
Manpower and population	0·618	0·729	0·753
Manpower growth and population growth	0·254	0·472	−0·070
Manpower and defence expenditure	0·923	0·747	0·421
Military participation ratio and defence burden	0·624	0·600	0·651
Defence expenditure per man and per capita GNP	0·705	0·841	0·649

Since the early 1960s, we have seen LDCs at all stages of this evolution. On gaining independence, for example, most of the African nations were firmly at the first stage, and the past decade has seen their progressive movement into the second. The continual warfare of the Middle East, and its association with the 'superpowers', places this region at the third stage, in common with Latin America whose military evolution has taken place over a much longer period. Finally, a handful of LDCs, such as China, India and Indonesia, appear to be able to move into the final stage, although it is clear that they are by no means committed to such a movement at present.

Any nation in one of the first two stages will naturally find itself increasing the demand for military manpower as the defence budget expands, as the technical relationship between labour and other inputs such as capital equipment will remain largely unaltered. Defence expansions will typically take the form of, say, increasing the size of the infantry, or expanding the existing tank corps with similar weaponry – both of these decisions will necessitate corresponding rises in military manpower. To a lesser extent, this is also true of the third stage, although here we should anticipate that capital-intensive technology would gradually force out labour. Such forcing-out would, of course, be relative and some absolute increase in manpower requirements could still be expected in general. It is only at the final stage, where conventional warfare is to be replaced by nuclear, that we find the technical role of labour considerably diminished, so that a net contraction of the armed forces is likely to occur as the defence budget expands. We should, incidentally, also anticipate that this process of capital intensification would also change the type of labour skills which the military demands.

A nation's selection of the appropriate level of military technology will naturally be determined by, amongst other things, the form of warfare in which it believes it is likely to become engaged. For this reason, very few nations have *totally* committed themselves to the final technological stage (the USA is possibly the sole example) as the conventional form of warfare seems the more probable, particularly in the Third World case. In addition, it could reasonably be asserted that, in times of crisis, a nation is more likely to remain at its particular stage and expand its existing forces, rather than attempt to change stages in the middle of a conflict. We should, in other words, anticipate an increase in defence spending during conflicts, accompanied by an expansion of military manpower – Israel, Iraq and Uganda are examples.

Such theories regarding military expenditure lead us to anticipate a relationship between the military participation ratio and the defence burden – the greater the military expenditure, the more manpower will be required. Indeed, our correlation coefficients do suggest such a conclusion.

Our final relationship, between defence expenditure per man and per capita income, also lends support to our previous arguments relating to military technology. The strong correlation is consistent with the facts that (i) military technology in the higher-income countries is more capital-intensive, i.e., at a 'higher' stage, and (ii) the wages paid to soldiers are a positive function of per capita income. Relating this correlation to observations as the nature of the predominant military technology throughout the world, we should conclude that, all other things remaining equal, richer countries have richer soldiers, employed in relatively more capital-intensive military technology.

The values of expenditure per man range from around an average of $31,000 for NATO, through around $16,000 for WTO and the Middle East, down to $8000 and below from the rest of the world. Clearly, to prove the 'capital-intensity' argument we require data on wage rates, which is difficult to obtain, especially for LDCs. However, on the assumption that a proxy for wages might be per capita national income, we may clearly see that the DC militaries are much more capital-intensive than those of the nations of the Third World. This point is reinforced by the likelihood that the wages of the LDC armed forces are higher than per capita income. Because the defence allocation comes from the central government, wage payments are better documented and more accurate than the crude estimates made for other sectors of LDC economies, such as subsistence agriculture. The averaging procedure will naturally be weighted by the low values of money income of the latter groups, implying that the LDC value for military capital per man must be even lower than was first suggested.

If our theories of manpower growth are correct, how do we explain the instances of decline of manpower levels over the past few years? A number of nations appear to have adopted defence policies which do not fit in with our model as presented above, although statistical discrepancies do explain some instances – in Laos, for example, the Royal Lao Army of the early 1970s has been disbanded and has been replaced by the Lao People's Liberation Army, a smaller force. In such cases, the growth rate is not measuring the same armed force over time.

On the other hand, several manpower declines have been engineered by deliberate policy changes. Portugal has seen a progressive demobilisation of troops since its withdrawl from its former colonies in Africa, and this policy also reflects the anti-militaristic stance of the present government. In the case of Zaire, the army has shed a considerable number of men in order to permit resources to be allocated towards the development of the air force. In Colombia, too, the navy and air force have both grown at the expense of army manpower. In both of these cases, defence expenditure growth has been less than income growth, i.e., there has been a proportional contraction of the defence sector, and economies have therefore been necessary to attain the desired policy objectives.

Our participation ratio data indicate that, on average, slightly under one per cent of the world's population is employed in the defence sector. This figure does not present a completely accurate picture of labour involvement, however, for two reasons.

First, in addition to the regular forces whose numbers are presented in Table 3.1, many nations possess large para-military organisations which, although not classified as military groups, perform similar functions and require equipment from additional expenditures. Brazil, for example, possesses 200,000 para-military personnel in addition to the 270,000 regular troops. In other cases, substantial 'reservist' armies exist and such 'part-time' soldiers also require equipment and training facilities. Pakistan, for example, possesses a reservist army of half-a-million, and this exceeds its regular army in size. Such organisations and armies predominate in those nations which are experiencing, or believe that they are about to experience, conflicts, and, in general, a large para-military reflects the scale of the internal disruptions, whilst a substantial reserve army reflects the scale of potential international aggression. Additional examples of the former instance are South

Africa and Ethiopia, whilst Egypt and Israel are instances of the latter.

Secondly, the simple participation ratio does not portray a particularly useful picture from the economic point of view as it does not distinguish between *types* of labour. In general, the most productive labour within an economy tends to be the male 18–45 age-group, and it is also from just this group that the armed forces are recruited. This being so, the figure of 4.5 per cent of the Israeli population being in the armed forces really implies that some 24 per cent of the economically most active section of the workforce is being displaced from civilian production. A proportion of this order also holds for other LDCs, in spite of their lower participation ratios – the percentage of the male 18–45 group in military service in Egypt is 4.4 per cent, in Pakistan 4.0 per cent, and in Uruguay also 4.4 per cent.[5]

This being so, we must now pose the question – does the military sector, which employs several per cent of the active labour force, absorb labour which could potentially be used in more socially-productive civilian enterprises? To answer this, let us examine the nature of LDC economies.

A major factor in the economic development of the Third World is not the shortage of labour but the problem of labour absorption.[6] In terms of the input requirements for capacity output, the majority of LDCs are experiencing a labour surplus. This is not solely due to the slow growth of output, but also the increasing preference on the part of the entrepreneurs for capital-intensive production techniques. This state of affairs has been the case ever since the end of the Second World War. Whilst LDC industrial output grew at over 7 per cent per annum for the period 1948–61, industrial employment grew at only 3.5 per cent per annum for the same period. Third World populations are characterised by strong rural-to-urban migration trends, owing to the attraction of city life, higher wages and the poor prospects in the agricultural sector. These factors account for the growth of LDC urban populations at a rate of 4.6 per cent per annum during the period, and a steady increase in urban unemployment is indicated. Latin America's problems were particularly acute at the time, the annual growth rate of the urban populations reaching of 5.6 per cent for the 1950s. By the early 1960s, and in spite of an excellent record of GNP growth, over 15 per cent of the Venezuelan labour force was unemployed. The situation in Africa has been much the same – a number of countries, such as Kenya, Malawi and Zambia, have actually experienced negative growth of industrial employment, despite substantial increases in industrial output.

At the present time, unemployment has reached relatively high levels in many regions of the world – DCs and LDCs alike are currently suffering from an excess of labour – and Table 3.3 illustrates this for a sample of 6 DCs and 11 LDCs. It should be borne in mind that these data relate only to persons registered as unemployed. Whilst the DC estimates are therefore reasonably accurate, the LDC figures are usually regarded as an underestimate of the true situation. This is due to the difficulties attached to the registration process in such countries (e.g. illiteracy) and also to the problems of defining unemployment in those nations where subsistence production is in preponderance. Indeed, the UN data record that, whilst the overall unemployment figure for Chile is around 3 per cent, a more realistic estimate for the number of persons without a job in the Santiago area is currently 15 per cent.

TABLE 3.3 Unemployment rates in 6 DCs and 11 LDCs, 1975, expressed as the percentage of registered unemployed in the total registered labour force. An asterisk indicates a 1974 figure

Country	Unemployment Rate
Australia	4·4
Britain	4·5
German FR	4·7
Japan	1·9
Italy	3·3
USA	8·5
Argentina	2·3
Bolivia	3·7
Egypt	2·3*
Israel	3·1
S. Korea	4·1
Nicaragua	7·3*
Panama	6·1
Peru	4·9
Philippines	4·2
Syria	4·8
Uruguay	8·1*

Source: UN (1976), Table 22, pp. 89–92.

Given these facts, our initial observation must therefore be that, regarding labour in general, it is most unlikely that the military absorbs the manpower resources required for civilian usages, as there exists a considerable pool of unemployment in most LDCs, irrespective of the level of military demand.

It is, however, important to distinguish between differing types of labour. It would seem likely that urban unemployment is largely due to the lack of skills on the part of the unemployed workforce, and it is just this skilled and educated labour that is in short supply in the Third World. Demand for this type of labour should therefore be correspondingly high. It would therefore be instructive to examine the employment possibilities of educated labour to determine whether the military is siphoning off such scarce resources from potentially more productive areas.

French and Boyd (1971) undertook a survey to examine the employment opportunities for school-leavers in Ghana. By LDC standards, such people should be well qualified to enter almost any field of public or private sector employment. Educational investment in Ghana is high relative to world standards – around 25 per cent of the 1960s budgets went to education – and this would lead us to anticipate a reasonably able labour force. In theory, Ghanaian education is designed to provide preliminary preparation for careers whose specialist nature will require specialist training.

When French and Boyd came to examine the institutions which regularly employed school-leavers, they discovered that the demand was surprisingly low. For the year mid-1968 to mid-1969, less than one-half of the firms interviewed replied that they employed a substantial number of leavers; the remainder apparently had little use for this type of person. The firms which were keenest to employ the school-leavers were banks and public services although the demand, in absolute terms, lagged considerably behind supply. In total, for the area surveyed, only 2600 vacancies existed for 3000 qualified persons. As the area was predominantly industrial, the results possibly present the most optimistic picture of LDC employment. It should be borne in mind, however, that Ghana is, to some extent, a special case in that its educational throughput is higher than that of many other LDCs. In nations which devote less resources to education, skilled labour is correspondingly more scarce. Even so, as Table 2.4 has shown, education is a primary spending priority for much of the Third World, leading us to anticipate that skilled labour will became more plentiful in the future. It might well then encounter similar problems as those met by unskilled labour at present.

Unemployment of skilled labour has other dimensions, as Peil (1969) shows in another study of Ghana, in the region of Tema. Her analysis suggests that unemployment of skilled labour might also come about as a result of the structural deficiencies in the economic system. Tema was developed during the 1950s and 1960s as a port and an industrial site, and this served to attract large numbers of skilled labourers from all parts of the country. However, the completion of all the major construction schemes has left many of these people without employment, as the factories mainly employ unskilled labour for routine or supervisory tasks. Peil's survey reveals that this labour force is unwilling to move from Tema, not only owing to family commitments, but also, and more importantly, because their

awareness of widespread unemployment makes them question the wisdom of leaving their contacts to start again elsewhere. (p. 419)

McQueen (1969) has examined the implications of the educated unemployed for the socio-political environment. His study of Nigerian school-leavers indicates that (i) most school-leavers are anxious to attain status and occupational careers in a 'modern' context, (ii) most school-leavers tend to be optimistic about the prospects of finding such employment. Those persons disaffected about the system, McQueen argues, are 'socially marginal' – they are a numerical minority and are not sufficiently organised or defined to represent a coherent interest group. McQueen was particularly concerned to refute the notion that such disaffected school-leavers constituted an immediate political problem. However, some Third World governments have seen the issue as being more urgent, as we shall see later.

The conclusions to be drawn from such evidence are clear. Firstly, manufacturing industry does not require a substantial amount of labour in that it favours capital-intensive production. This implies that it prefers to employ a smaller number of lower-paid semi-skilled persons in an operative capacity. Furthermore, the public and tertiary sectors, whilst demanding labour of both the skilled and unskilled type, cannot produce a demand large enough for total resource utilisation. By way of substantiation, French and Boyd found a desire on the part of many students to continue on into higher education, in view of their poor employment prospects. We might therefore deduce that the military demand for labour can only produce the most minimal detrimental effect on the development effort in that a substantial surplus of labour is in continuous existence.

Because of this situation, recruitment has not presented much of a problem to the armies of the Third World; indeed, many of French and Boyd's students were opting for a military career. The military life-style is an added advantage:

> A soldier's life is regarded as providing steady employment in a society in which it is not easily obtained, and a standard of living above the average, along with the possibility of a 'position of responsibility', if only as the licensee of a petrol station, after a career of moderate distinction in the ranks. (Gutteridge, 1965, PP. 76–7)

As a source of employment in its own right the military is a popular choice with the result that many LDC armies of a professional orientation are at liberty to be highly selective in their choice of applicants. Evidence of this is supplied by the results of Whyte's study of Peru (in Harbison and Myers, 1965). A questionnaire was set for a number of Lima high-school students to discover their preferences for future occupations. Out of the 25 selections offered, a military career was ranked second only to engineering. As Whyte observes:

> The great popularity of military careers for public schoolboys is particularly noteworthy. For some time, the military has provided the channels of social mobility for those who do not find favourable opportunities in other fields. . . The figures not only show a preference among many young men for power positions as opposed to economically productive positions; they also suggest that there remains the difficult problem in providing avenues of mobility in fields that would contribute to the growth of the economy. (p. 63).

Financial aspects are also significant in making the military profession appear attractive, as recent DC studies have confirmed. For example, in his recent analysis of UK recruitment behaviour, Withers (1977) concludes that relative wages and the prevailing unemployment situation are major influences upon the supply of recruits who make themselves available for military employment. Given the relatively high wages paid to LDC soldiers (cf. Lofchie's Uganda study) and the high unemployment levels in these countries, the demand for military employment should accordingly be high.

We have therefore seen that, whilst the military sector is successful in attracting labour due to the professional benefits offered, it is unlikely to drain off a significant quantity of resources in view of the general excess supply of both skilled and unskilled labour. Indeed, the military could have an important role in providing a solution to the problems arising from such a surplus. Several LDCs have already appreciated that the armed forces provide an effective means for harnessing under-utilised labour, and this important aspect of military strategy impinging upon development policy will be examined in a later chapter.

EDUCATION

Of our sample of 91 nations (Tables 2.3 and 3.2), two-thirds currently operate some form of conscription, or obligatory national service. Terms of service vary from country to country – whilst Switzerland requires all males of military age to undertake a few weeks' training each year, Egypt requires a three-year block. Of all regions, conscription appears to be the least popular in Africa where, in over half of the nations in our sample, military service is voluntary.[8] We have reason to believe, nevertheless, that military service will be popular here for the reasons outlined above.

In most countries, therefore, labour will enter the armed forces and remain there for a period of time before re-entering civil society. Depending upon the particular recruitment or conscription conditions, some individuals will naturally remain in service longer than others, but a considerable net throughput is bound to occur in all cases. Throughout this period of military service, the soldier will be subjected to a variety of forms of education and training which could be of potential use to the civil economy. We must therefore ask – does the military provide an educational service to extend the skills of the population?

Our initial task is to examine the nature of military education. At this stage, it is important to distinguish between the educational system for officers and that which is experienced by the rank and file. This is necessary, not only because the nature of the education differs, but also because it is the officer class which constitutes the permanent or semi-permanent element of the military sector. Elite education is more technical but, as it does not directly impinge upon the civil economy, it is not really germane to the issue at this stage.

It is clearly amongst the DCs that training in the military has been most developed. DC militaries have a professional orientation and are therefore obliged to compete for labour with other occupations. To take an example from the UK defence policy:

Everything possible will be done to make life in the services sufficiently attractive to compete successfully in all respects with civilian employment; and to enhance the status of military service in national life. (Cmnd. 4521, 1970, p. 9)

One method of competition is the provision of training facilities for recruits which allow them to obtain recognised qualifications whilst in military service, qualifications which will be of value on leaving the armed forces. Again, the Ministry of Defence in the UK has made numerous agreements with various trades unions such that qualifications obtained during military service will be recognised by those trained under normal civilian auspices. Naturally, the type of education offered will be determined by the military, rather than the civilian, requirements, but this still permits plenty of scope in the fields of technology, engineering and surveying, down to the more mundane but equally important aspects of military life, such as catering and administration.

Third World nations are generally unable to offer such a high or wide degree of training to their recruits. Indeed, the whole notion of training is modern in origin – it started with the expenditure expansion after the Second World War, and accelerated with an upsurge after 1960. In one way, the Second World War assisted the development effort of the LDCs – 500,000 Africans were mobilised and most were given rudimentary training, whilst a proportion received specialist education for machine maintenance and technical skills. After the war, training continued but the level of output was low. For example, during the late 1950s, the Pakistan army's apprentice school was only turning out 250 qualified technicians per year. In that the military's demand for trained personnel was high, the number of persons liberated for civil employment was correspondingly diminished.[9] In more recent times, because of the desire on the part of the military to attain some degree of self-sufficiency, the armed forces have found it necessary to train men in a variety of occupations for the day-to-day running of service organisations. Accordingly, cooks, clerks, managers and other service tradesmen will be trained to meet the army's needs and may eventually prove beneficial to the civil economy on demobilisation.

The experience of Burma provides interesting illustrations.[10] In 1961 the Defence Services Institute, formerly concerned with the procurement of army supplies, was expanded to include the Burma Economic Development Corporation. This entailed military responsibility for commercial enterprises such as steel production, shipping and also pharmaceuticals. The net result was a pool of trained entrepreneurs whose potential was clearly applicable above and beyond the military sector. The coup of 1962 made this policy even more urgent. The military government was considerably more left-wing and development-orientated than its predecessor, and it outlined a national plan along the following lines: (i) elimination of foreign control of Burmese resources by nationalisation; (ii) internal self-sufficiency and diminished reliance upon foreign markets; (iii) industrialisation and a fall in the dependence on the rice economy; (iv) centralisation and control of markets. Over the past decade and a half, some success has been exhibited in the attainment of these goals. Since the major posts of the country's bureaucracy were filled by military men, it would suggest that the military's training is most amenable to civilian application. We shall return to the case of Burma, and other examples of the type, in a subsequent chapter.

One especially important attribute of the military is its organisational structure; as observers have pointed out, it often represents the only 'modern' sector of an LDC economy. Lucien Pye (in Johnson, 1962) has noted that the military has a major role to play in the *modernisation* process.

> The term 'modernisation' refers to those social relationships and economic and technological activities that move a social system away from a traditional state of affairs in which there is little or no 'social mobilisation' among its members. More specifically, the term 'modernisation' refers essentially to those peculiar socio-economic institutions and political processes necessary to establish a cash nexus, in place of a feudal or social obligatory system, as the primary link relating people to each other, and to the social system, in the production of goods and services and in their exchange. (Kilson, 1963, pp. 426–7)

The armed forces of the Third World have tended to emphasise a rational outlook because, Pye believes, of their exposure to contemporary Western military technology. The 1940s/1950s type of Western army has served as a model for many Third World militaries.

> In so doing they have undertaken to create a form of organisation that is typical of and peculiar to the most highly industrialised civilisation yet known. Indeed, modern armies are essentially

industrial-type entities. Thus the armies of the new countries are instinct with the spirit of rapid technological development. (Pye, in Johnson, 1962, p. 76)

This is particularly true of the officer classes, who have to be trained in advanced industrial skills because their operations are technically demanding.

Pye goes on to advance other reasons for the 'modernity' of the armed forces. The army as a professional body sees its sphere of operation as external to the parent society – the soldier compares his organisation with that of foreign powers and competition exists within this framework. Furthermore, few LDC militaries have had to cope with everyday problems because they were created to deal with as yet unarisen future contingencies. They can therefore devote their energies to evolving towards the Western 'ideal' type.

The army, then, can provide the process by which traditional ways of life give way to Western practices. Even at the beginning of his career, the soldier has to break down his family ties and to adjust to an impersonal world. Because of the security offered by the military way of life, the soldier is better adapted to make this 'modernising' transition than, say, the peasant villager, and he therefore stands a greater chance of success. The very nature of the army organisation entails a degree of rationality and discipline and it is concerned quite specifically with means–ends relationships. As such, it stands out amongst the traditional institutions of the Third World.

For societies in the process of modernisation, changes in values and cultural orientations are of the utmost importance for advances in industrialisation and development. It is true that not all LDCs accept modernisation as an attribute of the type of social structure they wish to adopt – nevertheless, the modernising ideal is common to many nations of the Third World group. During the transition from a 'folk' to an 'urban' culture, a process described in a variety of ways by social theorists, a modernising agent will play a dominant role. Suffice it to say, the military represents the major, and possibly the only, 'Gesellschaft' element in the predominantly 'Gemeinschaft' LDC society and, by means of the dissemination of its ideology with labour throughput, will contribute towards the process of cultural development.[11]

From the experiences of a number of nations, such as Burma and Indonesia, it is clear that the armed forces are capable of both engaging in business activity and creating entrepreneurs. It could be argued, however, that the military is a causal factor in entrepreneurial shortages, in that the potential entrepreneurs might opt for an army career in preference to a business occupation. 'Enterprise' is in short supply in the nations of the Third World, and the prospective entrepreneur suffers from many handicaps – capital is scarce and there is a general ignorance of the market. Indeed, this very market is usually dominated by established firms, often of foreign origin, so that new entries are discouraged. In aggregate, a lack of business education exists. To blame the military for the withdrawal of this scarce resource – enterprise – seems unjustified. In the first place, the actual number of potential entrepreneurs who actually enter the armed forces must be minimal and those that do should, because of the potential for military enterprise, find their vocation in some such aspect of military service. However, the debate must remain conjectural owing to the difficulties involved in quantifying entrepreneurial activities. Nevertheless, it would seem reasonable to suggest that the modernisation and the education functions of military service outweigh any detrimental effects caused by the possible restrictions of enterprise.

ECONOMIC GROWTH

The empirical analysis of the mutual relationship between defence and the economy is, as we have seen, a complex exercise. Few major studies have therefore been attempted and many of our inferences have to be drawn from an 'intuitive grasp' of the situation. One significant exception to this generalisation is the valuable contribution of Benoit (1973) and an analysis of this work forms the substance of this section.

The first step in Benoit's study was the compilation of a viable data bank – he employed a sample of 44 LDCs considered over the period 1950-65. The relevant material – information relating to both the defence sector and the overall economy – was derived from UN, IBRD, IMF and AID sources in order to make the sample internally consistent. Preliminary analysis indicated that the growth of defence expenditure had been outstripping GNP growth over the period, and that the distribution of defence burdens throughout the world was primarily related to the requirements of military strategy – those nations with high proportionate levels of defence spending were either actually engaged in warfare or were located in potential confrontation areas, e.g. Yugoslavia and Burma.

Econometric analysis in the form of stepwise regression estimates for all the principal variables was then performed on the data. The most important conclusion is described by Benoit as follows:

> The big surprise of this study was the finding that the evidence does not indicate that defence has had any net adverse effect on growth in developing countries... The crucial evidence in this matter was the finding that the average 1950–1965 defence burdens (defence as a per cent of national product) of 44 countries was positively, not inversely, correlated with their growth rates over comparable time periods i.e., the more they spent on defence, in relation to the size of their economies, the faster they grew – and vice versa. This basic correlation was strong enough so that there was less than one chance in a thousand that it could have occurred by accident. (p. xix)

The major emphasis of the remainder of the study therefore became directed towards discovering the direction of causality between the two variables; in other words, was the correlation between defence and economic growth spurious?

Benoit deduced that defence expenditure had both adverse and favourable effects upon the possibilities for economic growth. On the negative side, he identified three different types of adverse effect. First, it is clear that growth might be limited because the defence establishment might take over resources which would otherwise be employed as civilian investment. In addition, it is likely that these resources would have served as a significant stimulus to economic growth in view of their nature – the military tends to require capital equipment, machine tools, metallic raw materials, foreign exchange, and so on. The case of India is cited to suggest that 50 per cent of this country's defence programme occurred directly at the expense of the civil investment allocation. Secondly, Benoit argued that defence spending must have a deleterious effect on growth by virtue of the fact that the government sector in general, and the military sector in particular, exhibits no observable productivity increases – resources are therefore being transferred to a relatively unproductive sector. The third adverse effect was termed the 'income shift' – an increase in defence will simply lower the civil GNP, all else remaining equal, and will naturally tend to influence growth proportionately. Benoit calculated that the combined adverse effect came to around 0.25 per cent per year, i.e. growth rates of civil

GNP were reduced by this amount due to defence spending.

Turning now to the favourable effects of spending, Benoit identified a considerable number: the defence sector contributes towards manpower training, supplies basic infrastructure, undertakes socially useful research and development, provides a source of employment and may undertake 'civic action' programmes, all in addition to maintaining public order and security. By virtue of the strong positive correlation, it was concluded that these favourable effects must outweigh the adverse ones, although Benoit noted that the former are extremely difficult to quantify.

Benoit examined alternative hypotheses to explain his correlation between the growth in defence spending and the growth of the economies. First, because of the existence of supporting evidence, he doubted whether the correlation could be spurious. Secondly, he also believed that no systematic bias existed in the data, and therefore this could not be an explanation of the result. There existed little evidence to suggest that it was economic growth which was causing the expansion in defence – changes in burdens occurred at random and were not correlated with rises in government revenues. Indeed, variations seemed to be best explained, as always, by strategic and planning considerations. Benoit's final assertion was that defence spending *must* have some positive effect on economic growth, coupled with the influence of international economic aid and domestic investment. However,

> the statistical evidence is highly ambiguous – it neither lends strong support to our hypothesis nor does it really undermine it. General and qualitative considerations derived from our research lead us, nevertheless, to suppose that the hypothesis is likely to be correct. (p. 24)

We have already examined much information to suggest that Benoit's assertion that defence spending can play an enhancing role in the development process does contain a great deal of truth and, indeed, more recent studies have replicated Benoit's results. In his analysis, Kennedy (1974) reviewed a large number of LDCs and concluded that:

> The growth rates for GDP of individual countries did not seem to have been affected by their defence allocations. (p. 188)

For our own particular sample (Table 2.3), we find a strong correlation between defence expenditure growth and per capita income growth – the correlation coefficients are 0.649 for DCs and 0.496 for LDCs – although this can partially be explained by virtue of the inherent inflationary trends within each series. The relationship between defence burden and per capita income in LDCs is as predicted by Benoit – the correlation coefficient is 0.224 – but the figure for the DC sample is negative (−0.355). This DC coefficient accords well with the results of the study by Smith (1977) who used mid-1960s data for a sample of fifteen capitalist nations. The burden/growth coefficient in this case was −0.54 and Smith explains this by postulating that defence spending and investment are mutually conflicting claims on resources. To take a final LDC instance, Weidenbaum (1974) notes that a Rand Corporation study of Latin America suggests that nations with larger arms expenditures possess faster-growing economies.[12]

Unfortunately, statistical correlations do not, in themselves, provide the answers to the main questions – does defence expenditure cause economic growth or does such growth permit more defence spending? We can reason, however, that both propositions are likely to be true, depending upon particular circumstances. Nations such as Saudi Arabia, Iran and Kuwait, with rapid economic growth brought about by their oil revenues, can naturally afford to expand their armed forces with little deleterious effect upon their economies. Again, the high growth of the South African economy during the 1960s provided resources for the expanding domestic military budget and the weapons imports from Britain and France.

On the other hand, the evidence of this chapter does suggest that the defence sector will generate some economic growth of its own accord and, as a final example, let us consider the case of Pakistan. In his study of that country, Ahmad (1972) notes that the early 1950s were a period of exceptionally high defence spending and this growth was due, to a large extent, to internal military pressure and the possibility of conflict with India. At this time, defence accounted for around 70 per cent of the national budget each year, yet, in spite of the strain that this imposed upon the availability of finance, Ahmad notes that:

> The huge defence expenditure contributed enormously to the growth of West Pakistan's economy by way of establishing varieties of defence industries and an extensive network of transport and communication facilities. This gave income and

employment opportunities to her people. The persistent demand for a wide range of goods and services for military purposes gave rise to a large number of contractors, traders and manufacturers, which led to the growth of a vast number of ancillary activities. (p. 67)

Interestingly enough, this defence-led expansion appeared to give rise to a 'Defence-Business Lobby' in politics, an extremely embryonic military-industrial complex. When the post-Korea depression hit Pakistan, the government felt obliged to deflate the economy by expenditure cutbacks but came under pressure from this particular group. Fortunately for this government, the USA chose this time to offer substantial military assistance to Pakistan.

THE COST OF DEFENCE EXPENDITURE

Throughout this chapter we have reviewed a number of areas relevant to a discussion of the economic costs of defence. In most instances, we have discovered that defence spending induces beneficial economic effects. Even so, the fact remains that the military sector absorbs an enormous quantity of resources. It was mentioned earlier that the world's defence allocation exceeded $300 thousand million; here are some additional dimensions:

(i) The world defence expenditure total for 1977 exceeded the combined national outputs of the nations of Africa, South Asia and the Far East;

(ii) this annual defence expenditure is approximately equal to the sum spent by the nations of the world on education and public health combined;

(iii) the total world allocation to defence during the decade of the 1960s exceeded $2 trillion. This was equivalent to the world devoting the combined national outputs of France and the United Kingdom to defence over the same period.[13]

It is hardly surprising to find that such facts have caused anxiety to both politicians and economists alike, for the central point remains that $300 thousand million represents a tremendous amount of resources and, accordingly, a very high opportunity cost. Indeed, the United Nations has been concerned with this issue for a number of years. Its reports are specifically concerned with the ways in which resources could have been used to accelerate wider economic development by investment in both capital and labour. With particular reference to the DCs, who are the largest defence spenders, it notes that funds could have been provided to improve the environment, to benefit the Third World, and to expand research in socially useful areas such as medicine, population studies and agriculture.[14]

The costs of defence spending are not purely economic. As the UN has made clear, increases in spending merely serve to enhance the instability of international politics by increasing the social tensions between nations. Furthermore, the stockpiling of weapons of war, to the point of 'overkill' and beyond, accompanied by the neglect of the welfare of millions of persons throughout the world, is a strong factor in the disillusionment of substantial proportions of the populations of many societies. In addition, with respect to the internal situation, the changing balance between the military and the civil economy can be seen as a potential threat to democracy.

Several writers have turned their attention to those goals which might be better accomplished if resources could be diverted from the military sectors. For example, Benoit (in Benoit and Boulding, 1963) has compiled a personal list of 'social priorities' for the USA during the 1960s, the cost of which is roughly equal to the defence allocation. His programme would include steps to end serious poverty, industrial investment, the expansion of welfare services, urban renewal, research and development and the extension of the foreign aid programme.

The case of the UK during the 1960s is also of interest. In its appraisal of the possibilities of attaining a 4 per cent growth rate of economic output, the National Economic Development Council (NEDC, 1963) observed that the major determinant would be the availability of investment resources. It was estimated that a further 2 per cent of GNP would have to enter the investment sector from some source or other; at this time, the defence budget was running at 6.5 per cent of GNP. The actual growth achieved during the 1960s was 3 per cent per year, held back by the unavailability of investable resources. This experience serves to demonstrate the growth potential inherent in the resources devoted to the defence sector, a growth potential which could be realised by their reallocation.

The most ambitious attempt to value the true opportunity costs of defence expenditure is that undertaken by Benoit and Lubell (in Benoit, 1967). In their analysis, the authors take into account not only the levels of expenditure and the resulting opportunities forgone, but also the economic benefits of spending of the types which we have discussed in earlier sections. The initial model was based upon data for the USA in the mid-1960s although, using material for other nations, it may be generalised to permit estimations for other regions of the world. The technique is as follows.

Defence expenditure can be disaggregated into its major components – expenditure on personnel, capital equipment, research and development (R&D), construction, operating costs and transfers abroad, although the last-mentioned is insignificant and will be ignored for our present purpose. Of these, the expenditure on personnel and equipment represent direct costs in the sense that this form of activity is completely specialised, bearing no relationship to the civilian economy. The costs of personnel therefore represent the loss to civil production caused by the very fact of military employment, measured as the product of manpower and the average civil wage rate. Military capital, on the other hand, is costed at face value.

R&D costs cannot be treated in such a simple manner owing to the possible existence of 'spin-off'. Benoit and Lubell estimated that, whilst 60 per cent of R&D was completely military-orientated, 40 per cent yielded potential civilian benefits and could not therefore be treated as a complete cost.

> Applying the US ratios, we reached the hypothetical conclusion that perhaps $4.6 billion of the world's $13.8 billion of defense R&D... was sufficiently similar to civilian R&D, or had the likelihood of enough identical payoff to the civilian economy, so that its inclusion in the defense program did not in reality reduce the resources available for pursuing the long term goals of civilian welfare. The gross opportunity cost of world defense R&D is thereby set at $9.2 billion. (Benoit, 1967, p. 52)

A similar procedure was applied to military construction, bearing in mind that some of the possible opportunity costs again did not exist owing to the civil usage of military resources, such as road and communications networks. It was estimated that 15 per cent of military construction had such civil applications. In the 'operating costs' category, allowance was made for the benefits of military education, training, medical services and housing.

From their calculations, Benoit and Lubell concluded that 11 per cent of the US military budget constituted a positive contribution to civil welfare. The remaining 89 per cent was labelled the 'gross opportunity cost', i.e., the total defence expenditure less any socially useful spending which produces civil benefits. Now, this 89 per cent only represents the full opportunity cost if it is believed that the appropriate amount of defence for the society concerned is zero. Given the current state of the world, zero defence seemed inconceivable and this factor led Benoit and Lubell to ask – what is the minimum expenditure required to maintain international and internal security? The final, net, opportunity cost is therefore the difference beween the gross cost and this minimum expenditure requirement.

Clearly, such a requirement is difficult to calculate as each nation will have its own views as to the appropriate level of security which is desirable. For their particular calculation, Benoit and Lubell chose to use a model developed by USACDA in 1962 which outlined the principles of an international security organisation whose cost was estimated to potentially run at some $21 billion each year. Allocating prospective contributions to this agency in proportion to current contributions to the UN, Benoit and Lubell were able to arrive at a final figure for net opportunity cost.

Working within this framework, it was estimated that 28 per cent of US expenditure was genuinely necessary for defence purposes, giving a net opportunity cost of 61 per cent of the defence budget. This sum is equivalent to around 5 per cent of the US GNP. For the 35 other nations also considered – mainly NATO and WTO countries – the net cost varied between 1 per cent and 3 per cent of GNP, at approximately the same proportionate level. The total net cost for the world was estimated as 62 per cent of defence expenditure, or, at that time, over $70 billion.

What are the consequences of such an analysis for the nations of the Third World? Benoit and Lubell did not attempt many estimations for the LDCs because of the lack of data, a problem which still exists at the present time. Some Middle Eastern nations were considered, but these results can hardly be relevant now owing to the sharp increase in the intensity of conflict in the area. The case of India was examined, with the conclusion that the net opportunity costs ran at around 2.5 per cent of GNP, or 55 per cent of the defence budget. The Third World, taken en bloc, yielded a net cost of 37 per cent of defence expenditures.

The basic assumptions of the model suggest, however, that some degree of modification is necessary before it can become fully applicable to the LDCs:

(i) The ratios used for the determination of that proportion of expenditure which has potential civil utility largely follows those established for the USA case. It is reasonable to suppose that these ratios will vary for different nations, especially those of the Third World.

(ii) The model assumes that the labour which the military employs could always be alternatively employed in the civil sector. This might not be true for LDCs which, as we have seen, generally experience high unemployment rates. If military manpower would not have been employed in such an alternative use, the opportunity cost of this resource becomes zero.

(iii) The model makes no allowances for the existence of a state of war; it assumes that peace is prevailing and that the function of defence is as a deterrent to the outbreak of war. In a warfare situation, minimum defence needs would naturally rise, as in the Middle Eastern case.

(iv) Many LDCs require expenditure for the control of internal instability. Benoit and Lubell have realised the implications of this factor:

> In the developing countries in general, further strengthening of national forces may be required to suppress tribalism, separatism, warlordism, local insurrections, and sheer anarchy. For the purpose of the rough estimate in hand, we have merely arbitrarily applied a one-sixth ratio across the board to estimate the 'minimal' internal defense programs. However,. . . in reality the proportions would undoubtedly vary considerably from country to country. (p. 56)

(v) As a general criticism, the whole model is, of course, completely conjectural and Benoit and Lubell are at pains to point this out. No analytical device exists which can accurately predict the correct level of military expenditure, although, as we have seen, military planners are now taking more steps in this direction. Indeed, the 'correct' level can only really be established in retrospect. The setting of any minimum for defence requirements must therefore remain a subjective decision. Even so, some such minimum must be posited for any analysis to take place at all.

(vi) Benoit and Lubell have omitted certain aspects from costs which could usefully be included in the Third World case. For we have seen that military industry can yield benefits, both of production for, and stimulation of, the civil market and n the regional multiplier effects. An important variable, although one not capable of quantification, is education and a modernisation ethic which the military can impart, an ethic which many theorists have seen as a prerequisite for development.

(vii) LDCs have very much smaller defence expenditures than larger nations, and we could reasonably expect that the resource wastage brought about by strategic 'overkill' affects them much less than it does the high-budget DCs.

These modifications mean that the ratio of 'necessary' to 'wasted' military expenditure is very different in the LDC cases, as a much greater proportion of the generally smaller defence budget provides either positive benefits or is necessary for strategic reasons. In other words, the estimated proportion of 37 per cent costs could reasonably be diminished even further and this would bring the average net cost for a non-warring LDC down to less than 1 per cent of GNP, although this mean value will possess a high variance. Comparing this to Benoit and Lubell's figures of around 5 per cent of GNP for the USA and the USSR, the 2–3 per cent for the European nations, we see that it is the DCs, and not particularly the LDCs, which really carry the heaviest defence burden. As a footnote, it is sobering to reflect that the mid-1960s defence costs for the DCs in aggregate represented over nine times their total allocation of international aid.

4 Military Trade and Aid

In addition to the purchase of domestically-produced military equipment, the payment of the armed forces and so forth, governments devote a considerable volume of resources to international arms flows. This chapter is concerned with this flow of defence-related resources between the DCs and the nations of the Third World; more specifically, it is concerned with military trade and aid. In theory, trade and aid can easily be distinguished: if goods or services are exchanged at a rate directed by the free operation of the market mechanism (or 'normal' commerce), then trade is occurring. Should these terms be modified to give benefits in favour of one participant, over and above those utilities anticipated from normal trading operations, then aid is being transferred from the 'loser' to the 'gainer'. However, as far as the military is concerned, the juxtaposition is not as straightforward as has been outlined above, and this may be seen from the examination of a taxonomy of possible international military transfers.

In terms of the transfer of capital, or claims upon capital, from DCs to the nations of the Third World, the following may occur:

(i) donation of military equipment to the LDC, often surplus to the donor's requirements,

(ii) direct financial grants to LDCs, for the purchase of military equipment, or to develop other military facilities such as training schools,

(iii) the granting of preferential terms for the purchase of equipment, such as credit arrangements or the permission to pay in local currency,

(iv) 'normal' trade at cost price.

With respect to labour, the DCs might:

(v) provide training facilities in a DC institution for selected members of the LDC armed forces,

(vi) Send military missions or experts to advise and train the LDC military, *in situ.*

For some of these possibilities, we can clearly distinguish between trade and aid. Item (i) must be considered as pure aid by any standard, assuming that no conditions are imposed upon the acceptance of the gift. However, in cases such as item (iii), there is an overlap between trade and aid, making such a transaction difficult to categorise. Even when an LDC actually buys equipment at the market price we cannot be certain that there is no aid element, as the purchase might be occurring on the basis of a previously-donated grant. For these reasons, we shall employ the term 'assistance' to cover all aspects of international transfers of resources, and disaggregation will be attempted wherever possible.

The main countries which provide military assistance in one form or another at the present time are the United States of America, the Soviet Union, the United Kingdom and France. Other suppliers, whose contributions are of much less significance in terms of value of exports, are West Germany, Italy, Canada, Sweden, Switzerland, the Netherlands, Japan and China. The recipients of such assistance are, by and large, the nations of the Third World.

By far the best index of military assistance is the data for the imports and exports of major weapons. For convenience, we shall term these transactions military 'trade'. In reality, this material forms the only significant data on assistance that has been accumulated and aggregated. Even so, it clearly possesses a number of deficiencies. It completely omits the labour aspects of assistance, the equipment donations, and also that proportion of the financial grants which is not spent on weapons imports. Trade in minor weapons is not included – transactions of this type are numerous but individually insignificant, with the result that they are seldom recorded in aggregate. Trade data will, however, be considered, and suggestions for modifications will be advanced as the argument proceeds.

Table 4.1 presents data on imports of major weapons by regions of the Third World. As will be seen, in order to provide additional information, Vietnam has been treated independently of the remainder of the Far East, and Africa has been subdivided into three areas. Unlike defence budgets and their annual trends, imports vary erratically from year to year, depending upon the LDC's requirements and the particular exporting policies of the supplier. With the exception of the data for 1976, five-year moving averages are presented as these tend to smooth

TABLE 4.1 Imports of Major Weapons by Region, 1956–76, expressed in $US million (1975 prices), as a five-year moving average (1976 – yearly figure). Items may not sum to totals owing to rounding

	1956	1960	1964	1968	1972	1976
Middle East	305	314	447	1087	1899	3614
South Asia	296	315	219	314	373	414
Far East	350	500	379	363	282	1038
Vietnam	22	51	107	387	467	—
North Africa	—	16	63	110	157	929
Sub-Saharan Africa	9	40	70	85	185	432
South Africa	33	14	100	67	99	118
Latin America	200	262	190	168	388	768
TOTAL	1219	1516	1574	2582	3853	7312

Source: Condensed from SIPRI (1977), Table 7E1, pp. 306–7.

such disturbances.

As may be seen, the annual volume of arms imports has risen rapidly over the past two decades – the increase has been almost six-fold as compared to the four-fold growth in Third World military expenditures. Such expansion, however, has not been common to all regions. South Asia, for example, appears to have continued to import approximately the same total each year, whilst the demands of the Middle East have escalated markedly.

Table 4.2 provides parallel data for the major exporters of weaponry to the Third World. During the 1950s, no one nation appeared to possess a real monopoly of the arms trade although, by 1976, the USA had clearly emerged as the major supplier. During the 1960s, the USSR stepped up its exports considerably but its dominance of the market was only temporary. The share of the two former imperial powers, Britain and France, has declined continually since the 1950s, although the total value of exports by these nations has, of course, increased.

Of the 'Rest of World' group, West Germany and Italy are the next most important suppliers although their share is clearly minute. China, on the other hand, *was* a significant exporter in the late-1950s. Trade *between* LDCs also occurs, some $200m being exported by such nations to other Third World countries in 1976.

TABLE 4.2   Exports of Major Weapons by Supplier, 1956–76, expressed as percentage share of total market. Export values expressed in $US million (1975 prices)

	1956	*1960*	*1964*	*1968*	*1972*	*1976*
USA	34	47	31	28	50	53
USSR	15	14	31	43	27	21
Britain	21	17	15	11	11	8
France	13	3	11	11	10	8
Rest of World	17	19	12	7	2	5
TOTAL VALUE	1253	1515	1194	2692	3508	7312

Source: Derived from SIPRI (1977), Table 7E2, pp. 308–9.

THE NATURE OF ASSISTANCE

At the beginning of this chapter, we saw that, in theory, assistance could take any one of a number of forms. In order to understand the practical side of the issue, we shall next consider the example of the USA, the major provider of military assistance.[1]

Table 4.3 presents a breakdown of US military assistance, including trade, over the past three decades. As may be seen, a number of categories exist, but the basic division is between the Foreign Military Sales Program (FMSP) and the Military Assistance Program (MAP). Let us consider the components of each.

The majority of official government arms sales are transacted by means of cash or credit. In the former case, which applies to most of the DCs, US military hardware is purchased directly on cash terms. However, if the purchaser does not have sufficient resources available for such a transaction, FMSP may advance credit, generally on favourable terms with relatively low interest rates and long repayment periods. In addition, FMSP may occasionally guarantee loans made by private financial institutions for weapons purchase and it may also sell production licences for the manufacture of US designed equipment in foreign countries.

The complementary programme, MAP, is primarily concerned with the distribution of grant aid, aid which is specifically intended for military purposes. The funds donated under MAP have been considerable and, individually, Taiwan, S. Korea, S. Vietnam

TABLE 4.3   US Military Assistance to Other Regions

	Middle East and South Asia	Far East	Africa	Latin America	Other DCs
FMS Cash Sales, 1950–72 ($m)	1,864	1,546	73	313	9,786
FMS Credit Sales, 1950–72 ($m)	2,153	462	53	377	110
Military Assistance Programme, 1946–70 ($m)	1,770	9,640	280	778	21,249
Training of foreign personnel, 1950–70 (thousands of men)	19	129	7	54	110
Value of naval vessels delivered 1946–70 ($m)	8	417	6	200	1,106
Value of 'surplus' weaponry, 1946–70 ($m)	43	551	17	63	606
'Food for Peace' Funds, 1946–70 ($m)	90	1,286	4	—	132

Source: NACLA (1972), p. 44, 57–8, 68, 80–2.

Greece, Turkey and several other DCs have been the major recipients. An important element of MAP is the military training programme, by which selected foreign personnel are provided with military education either in the USA or in their own countries.

Although FMSP and MAP constitute the central thrust of US assistance, resources have also been provided in many other ways. First, a number of US naval vessels have been offered to some nations on indefinite loan, notably to Taiwan, the Philippines, Greece and Turkey. Secondly, many domestic defence items which the USA came to regard as 'surplus to requirements' were delivered, mainly to S. Korea, Taiwan, Greece and Turkey. Thirdly, the 'Food for Peace' programme, whereby the USA exported surplus foodstuffs to the poorer nations, generated local currencies: the main beneficiaries were S. Korea and S. Vietnam.

In addition to the above items listed in Table 4.3, a few additional factors must be taken into account before we exhaust the range of US assistance. First, hardware and training are provided to many nations via a Police Assistance Program, a programme which specifically aims to assist the police or para-military in counter-revolutionary operations. Throughout the 1960s, some $280 million was spent in this manner, Thailand and S. Vietnam being the main recipients. Secondly, the figures presented so far have excluded the direct sales of military equipment by US *private* industry to other nations. The total commercial sales for 1962–69 have been estimated at around $3500 million. Thirdly, and particularly throughout the 1960s, funds were allocated from the domestic defence budget to allies and mercenaries in the Far East theatre of war; between 1946 and 1970, some $8000 million was allocated in this way. Finally, all of these estimates must be regarded as understatements, owing to the fact that several of these defence transactions are kept secret, presumably for reasons of national security. The data presented excludes, for example, some assistance to India and Israel and we can imagine that the allocations to these nations have not been insignificant.

The assistance budgets of other nations have been similar to that of the USA, if considerably smaller. During the mid-1960s, UK 'aid' averaged $67 million per annum, and fell into four major categories – training and technical assistance, loans for the purchase of UK equipment, supporting assistance of the US type, and outright gifts. Of these, the first-mentioned predominated. Much of the arms sales occurred in the private sector, and this is true for all of the supplying nations, with the obvious exception of the USSR. The private trade in armaments is surrounded by a great degree of secrecy and little statistical documentation exists.

France's military assistance is largely orientated towards training and technical assistance.

> In 1970, there were 1400 officers and non-commissioned officers (NCOs) acting as military advisors in the ex-French colonies in Sub-Saharan Africa. In addition, there were approximately 400 French officers and NCOs in Morocco, Algeria, Tunisia, Cambodia and Laos. Eight hundred Africans are trained in France each year. Recently, France has agreed to establish a flying school in Bou Sfer in Algeria; personnel from Libya, Morocco and Tunisia are also expected to attend. (SIPRI, 1971, p. 261).

Although we are not specifically concerned with this aspect of the problem, military assistance also takes the form of aid to those organisations which *oppose* the government of certain countries, the grants and equipment supplied being designed to accelerate the downfall of such regimes. The *Annual of Power and Conflict*

(Crozier, 1972) lists fourteen International Front organisations, whose role it is to advance the causes of Soviet or Chinese Communism, and 78 extremist movements of both left- and right-wing persuasions which are committed to the use of violence in the attainment of their ends. The source of such funds is naturally obscure, but Peking, Moscow, Washington and Havana appear to be prominent contenders. Equally, it is impossible to estimate the actual amount of the resource transfers to such organisations, and the evaluation of their economic contributions must be purely conjectural.

The variety of the possible types of assistance is therefore very wide. Why does it occur? There are a number of reasons for the giving and receiving of assistance, from the point of view of both participants. The DCs might wish to supply some form of assistance (i) to gain political or economic advantage and influence in the recipient nation, possibly at the expense of other potential suppliers, i.e. to enforce hegemony, (ii) to assist their own industry and export trade. On the other hand, the LDCs might demand assistance (iii) for the purposes of waging war, or to assist the domestic military effort in a war currently being waged, (iv) for prestige purposes, or to satisfy the military's desire for modernisation. These reasons will now be examined in more detail.

Hegemony. Although we take the term 'hegemony' to imply the general leadership, dominance and control by one nation over the affairs of others, there are really two distinct elements of the relationship.

First, US military escalation and assistance after the Second World War can be seen as an attempt to establish a political hegemony over the non-communist world, in opposition to competing claims from the communist bloc. Baran and Sweezy (1968), who analyse this issue in detail, see the events of 1947 as the catalyst which caused this process to begin. In this year, the Greek government was being threatened with the likelihood of a guerrilla takeover and UK support for the constitutional authorities was withdrawn. Declaring itself the protector of Greece and, indeed, of Turkey, the USA announced that:

it must be the policy of the United States to support free peoples who are resisting attempted subjugation by armed minorities or by outside pressure. (Quoted by Baran and Sweezy, 1968, p. 187)

The logical corollary of this, the Truman Doctrine, quickly became manifest. In order to assist in the major post-war reconstruction of the capitalist powers in Europe, the Marshall Plan was launched later in the same year. To develop the military counterpart to this economic policy, NATO was negotiated and finalised in 1949. The USA also began to take an interest in the remainder of the globe, signing a separate peace treaty with Japan in 1951 and establishing the basis of a military and economic assistance programme with that nation. Although NATO was to form the main multinational alliance, further treaties were concluded soon afterwards, possibly the most significant in the light of later events being the South-East Asia Collective Defence Treaty, which established SEATO in 1955. Finally, the USA entered into many bilateral defence agreements, and especially favoured those nations in close proximity – both geographically and, potentially, ideologically – to the Soviet bloc. Such nations came to be designated 'Forward Defence Areas' (FDAs).

Having undertaken this explicit commitment to act as the champion of the capitalist world, the USA was obliged to provide military assistance to its new allies, to add strategic credibility to its political sentiments. Throughout the 1950s and 1960s, NATO countries received substantial quantities of grant aid, Greece, Turkey, France (pre-1965) and Italy being amongst the major recipients. With regard to the FDAs, Thailand, Laos, S. Korea, S. Vietnam, Pakistan and Iran all received large shares of the assistance budget.

Throughout this period, the USA attempted to use the threat of withholding assistance as a method of control over its allies. Pakistan, for example, developed an increasing sympathy towards the socialist nations after the China/India conflicts of 1962, and the USA imposed two arms embargoes during the next decade. These were, however, largely ineffectual as the USSR, China and France were quite willing to provide the necessary equipment in place of the USA armaments. After this time, Pakistan/USA interests became further divorced; Pakistan left SEATO in 1973 and the organisation itself was formally terminated in 1977. Similarly, the USA reacted to the Greek coup of 1967 with the limitation of assistance, although this limitation was substantially relaxed after the Soviet invasion of Czechoslovakia.

With the US withdrawal from Vietnam at the end of the 1960s, it became clear that the original doctrine of Truman, reinforced by Kennedy, was no longer a realistic assessment of the US position – the

USA clearly would not commit itself *totally* to the suppression of communism. Indeed, defence policy in the post-Nixon era has been concerned with a much less overt form of military involvement. Whilst the USA has continued to supply increasing assistance to its former allies – mostly the nations of NATO, the FDAs and the Middle East – it appears to regard itself now as the facilitator of counter-insurgency rather than as the perpetrator.

The development of policy of the other major provider of assistance – the Soviet Union – was, in many respects, similar to that of the USA. Military assistance began in a small way as aid to N. Korea, but the strengthening of the NATO alliance necessitated the formation of the WTO in 1955 as a countervailing power. In addition, the USSR observed that it was being progressively encircled by nations under US hegemony and it reacted by attempting to find allies who were, as yet, 'uncommitted'. The Arab world was the first area to which overtures were made, whilst India and Afghanistan also became recipients of Soviet aid. Finally, the newly-independent nations of Africa, which the USA had largely excluded from its list of FDA regions of political importance, attracted Soviet interest during the 1960s.

As far as the LDC importers were concerned, the East/West arms competition of the 1950s and 1960s was highly desirable owing to the possibilities for bargaining which resulted. As we have already seen, the US withdrawal from involvement with Pakistan produced an immediate response from the other suppliers in the field. Iran also serves as an example for, in 1966, this country broke off negotiations with the USA relating to an oil-for-arms deal. Substantial amounts of Soviet equipment were thereafter purchased, and the USA reacted by agreeing to provide the desired weaponry as it was quite clear that Iran was prepared to alter its allegiances.[2] Indeed, it seems clear that a number of nations entered into alliances with the USA simply because of the possibility of being able to purchase sophisticated armaments on favourable terms.

At present, these possibilities of bargaining appear to be constrained by several factors. First, certain regions are regarded as being of minimal strategic importance to the 'superpowers' and the 'bidding' for influence in such areas will yield only poor returns to the LDCs concerned – the African region is an example, although political circumstances can certainly alter overnight. Secondly, many nations have already established themselves as being under a specific hegemony, either by treaty or by established tradition, and they are therefore of less interest to the major powers than are the non-aligned countries. Finally, the 'side-switching' which often results from using 'superpower' competition might result in a progressive loss of credibility and a decline in confidence on behalf of the assistance donors.

The second, and related, element of hegemony is economic dominance. DCs will, in other words, provide military assistance to nations in return for economic benefits. This variant of neo-imperialism is seen by many (and especially by Baran and Sweezy) as the major consideration involved in the provision of international military assistance. Thus France, for example, still supplies arms to its ex-colonies in Africa, in parallel to the maintenance of the more normal trading links. However, USA/Latin American relations possibly provide the clearest example.

During the 1960s, US private investment in Latin America was yielding an extremely high return. In this context, Arreas (1972) has noted that:

the United States receives from Latin America far larger sums than the investments that are realised. Between 1951 and 1963, it received 11.3 thousand million dollars as income from direct private investments in Latin America, while the investment during this same period amounted to only 5.7 thousand million. (p. 199)

In a particular instance – Chile in 1970 – Salvador Allende commented on the activities of the US-owned copper companies as follows:

Between 1930 and 1969, $3,700 million have left the country to increase the immense power of the international concerns which control copper deposits in five continents. In 1969, $166 million did not return. I must point out that $3,700 million is 40 per cent of the total wealth of Chile. . . (Allende, 1973, p. 79)

Given this form of economic structure in many Latin American countries, the strategy adopted by the USA was to send military assistance to these nations in order to counteract any actual or potential revolutionary activities which would destabilise the current government and therefore jeopardise US economic interests. A proportion of US assistance to this region is typically police aid and para-military equipment.

The pressure to export. In common with other industries, weapons production is susceptible to all the normal pressures of economic life. In the defence industries of the DCs, potential economies of scale exist, and it is naturally desirable to maintain the full usage of both capital and labour. In the longer term, evidence suggests that labour costs tend to fall owing to the 'learning' process.[3] Therefore, in view of these factors, and also the high initial R&D costs of producing a new weapon, an extended production run is necessary to recoup the investment.

However, although modern defence industries benefit greatly from high levels of output and long production runs, few DCs envisage sufficient expansion of their own defence programmes to allow for this. Exports therefore become of increasing importance to the DCs, if their scale of production is to be maintained and, in many instances, the sale of armaments overseas can be interpreted as a desire to develop the market, rather than to assert influence. This is certainly true in the case of recent UK policy.

The 1964–70 Labour Government in the UK made two particularly significant amendments to the British position on military matters. First, the domestic defence budget was continuously contracted to bring the UK's defence burden into line with the European norm, and, secondly, the political importance of assistance was superseded by the economic. During the 1950s, British arms diplomacy had been assisted by the empire but, with the independence of many such territories and their searches for new sources of weaponry, the UK influence declined considerably, as Table 4.2 has shown. Determined to halt this decline, in terms of value if not in terms of market share, the Labour Government tried to increase both trade and aid – Nigeria was a major market, although political pressure forced the UK to relinquish the lucrative South African market to France. However, significant export growth did not really occur until the 1970s when the Middle Eastern nations began to make major arms purchases. Of great importance for the UK industry was the 1976 Iranian order for over 1500 of the advanced 'Chieftain' tanks.

The needs of warfare. As in the case of domestic budgets, the primary cause for the demand for military assistance by the nations of the Third World is to meet the needs of warfare. It is, in fact, the strategic factor which appears to largely determine the level of arms imports, which themselves represent the greatest single element of assistance. This is shown by the analysis conducted by Kende (1972).

Kende was concerned with the proliferation of local wars in three

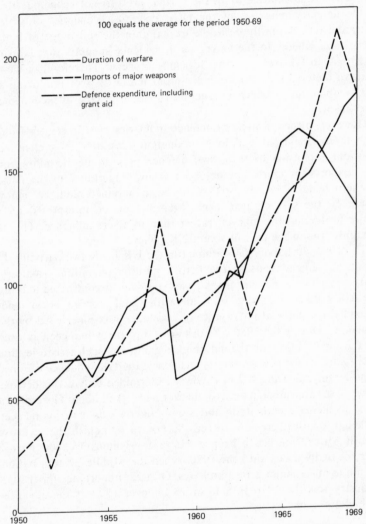

FIG. 4.1   Indices of War, Imports and Defence Expenditure for Third World Countries

Source: Kende (1972), Chart 7, p. 49.

regions of the world – Africa, Asia and Latin America. In the present context, his most interesting conclusions relate to the duration of warfare, military expenditures and the imports of weapons. The latter two categories are self-explanatory; they represent annual defence budgets including grant aid, and the value of arms imports received by the three continents respectively. The concept of 'war duration' involves the identification of wars – 93 occurred between 1945 and 1969 – and the estimation of the duration of each. For each particular year, we might therefore estimate the effective number of 'years' of actual warfare for the aggregate of the nations in the three continents under consideration. This variable can now be employed as a simple homoeomorphism of an 'intensity of war' function.

The results of Kende's analysis are illustrated in Figure 4.1. As we may see, the defence expenditure function follows a smooth upward trend, but the other two are subject to a high degree of variance about approximately the same mean. Nevertheless, they do exhibit something of a parallel tendency.

> When examining the aggregate figures. . . we find a really striking similarity between their trends, especially those in wars and arms imports. (Kende, 1972, p. 48)

Kende's intuitive conclusion is supported by regression analysis – the relationship between war and imports gives a coefficient of correlation of 0.821, and this figure increases slightly if imports are lagged by one year.

A Kende-type analysis can be applied to the Middle East for the period 1950 to 1970. In this region, imports display an upward time-trend, but the escalation of warfare significantly increases import demands. This is demonstrated by the following equation, which relates arms imports in any one year (M_t) to those of the previous year (M_{t-1}). Also included is a lagged dummy variable $(\text{Dum}_{t-1}$ which takes the value of unity in those periods when war actually occurs: 1950–2, 1956, 1958, 1967–70. It is thereby assumed that there will be a one-year lag between the demand for imports due to war and their receipt.[4]

$$M_t = 89.526 + 0.519\,(M_{t-1}) + 0.436\,(\text{Dum}_{t-1})$$
$$\quad\;\;(2.111) \qquad (2.053) \qquad\qquad (2.069) \qquad\qquad R^2 = 0.793$$

Although we cannot interpret these results as implying a direct causal linkage between imports and warfare, we can well understand the nature of such a relationship. Given a slowly-rising domestic expenditure trend, the announcement of a state of war will naturally imply a great increase in the demand for armaments and, indeed, for assistance in general. The internal economy will be unable to satisfy this increased demand in such a short space of time, and the country will therefore be driven to the purchase of armaments from elsewhere. In particular, DC arms will be demanded owing to their sophistication and, presumably, their efficiency. A time-lag is also to be anticipated in view of the prolonged nature of transactions, negotiations and transportation.

These relationships between conflict, weapons' imports and domestic defence budgets may also be discerned in the case of the South Asia region. Figure 4.2 illustrates the pattern of imports and military budgets between 1956 and 1976 and, in both cases, the trends are dominated by the policies of India, which is by far the largest military power in the region.

Once India had become independent (1947), her primary concern was to establish herself as the leading power in Southern Asia. This

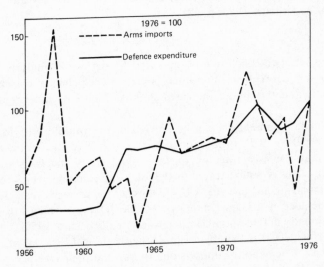

FIG. 4.2   Indices of Defence Expenditure and Arms Imports for South Asia, 1956–76

Source: SIPRI (1977), p. 222–3 and 306–7.

was considered especially urgent owing to fears of aggression from Pakistan, who had been receiving US assistance since the early 1950s. Defence policy was therefore orientated towards the development of immediate, tangible military strength, implying the rapid importation of jet aircraft, an aircraft carrier, warships and other equipment, mainly from the United Kingdom. In 1962, conflict broke out between India and China, necessitating further importation. However, Chinese supremacy served to destroy India's credibility – the equipment purchased proved unsuitable for guerilla-type border conflicts, and no back-up services had been provided for use with the weaponry. India therefore came to appreciate the need to expand her indigenous defence sector in more appropriate ways – domestic defence expenditure trebled in the next four years, and the reliance upon the outside world was diminished. Even so, India was still willing to accept assistance on more favourable terms – the UK and the USA together contributed over $US 140 million between 1962 and 1965, this total having a large 'aid' component. As we have seen, one aspect of India's policy was the establishment of a domestic defence industry. Assistance from the USSR was therefore particularly welcome, in view of the Soviet offer to develop three Mig aircraft assembly plants in India, staffed by Soviet technicians. Total Soviet aid during this period was roughly equivalent to the Western contribution.[5]

War with Pakistan in 1965 necessitated the further import of weapons, domestic expenditure again being unable to cope with the sharp rise in short-term demand. The level has been largely maintained, owing to the continual unrest in the area, i.e. the India–Pakistan–Bangladesh conflict and the Bangladesh coup.

In addition to the Middle East and India, Vietnam serves as another clear example for the increased demand for weaponry in times of conflict. Table 4.1 has already shown the large increases in imports over the past two decades, primarily associated with the major war which developed.

Prestige. Just as an established military sector is often considered by the Third World as the hallmark of an independent and flourishing nation, so sophisticated equipment can be considered as the hallmark of a modern armed force. Military assistance, in the form of the provision of modern weaponry, is therefore frequently in demand for prestige purposes.

Latin America will serve as an example in this instance. Two factors contribute to the increasing demand for sophisticated weapons in this region. Firstly, there exists inter-nation rivalry between the various militaries – if one state acquires a particular weapon, another feels obliged to obtain something similar or, preferably, superior. Brazil and Argentina have frequently competed in this way, in spite of the fact that there has been little potential hostility between the two nations. This rivalry developed some two decades ago when Brazil's imports rose from practically zero to over $US 60 million in 1955. Argentina replied with an importation of over $30 million in 1958, increasing to $40 million in 1960. Brazil's response was to import over $100 million in equipment in 1961.

An additional factor is inter-service rivalry. Typically, Latin American navies and air forces are recruited from the middle and upper classes in society, whilst the armies are predominantly lower-class. This has produced inter-class and intra-class competition. Again in Argentina, the 1958 naval expansion of $23 million produced a reaction from the army and air force by the purchase of $12 million and $24 million worth of equipment respectively. Conversely, the 1967 air force expansion of $18 million prompted a $23 million naval reply in 1968.[6]

The Latin American military sector occupies an important power position, with the result that demands for armaments are usually met. In many cases, the military itself actually forms the government, so that the procurement of weaponry presents less of a problem. This potential power of the army itself forms an important sub-reason for arms importation as we saw in the case of Uganda – major weapons were supplied to the army in an attempt to meet the army's desire for modernisation and thus to avoid the possibilities of military takeover.

THE COST OF TRADE AND AID

It might be argued that *technical* assistance – the training of personnel – produces beneficial economic effects upon the LDC economy, in the same manner as the military education aspect of domestic defence spending. This was one of the key observations of the US Presidential Committee set up to examine the military assistance programmes, and whose recommendations appeared in the 1959 'Draper Report'. This document indicated that the assistance programmes provided for the possibilities of education and civic action, a role which we shall examine subsequently. It was estimated that 300,000 persons had received training under MAP between 1950 and 1969. However, Windle and Vallence (1962) argued, in their evaluations of technical assistance, that the majority of training facilities were devoted to military ends, with no civil applications whatsoever. The nature of the training was also ideologically biased, one overt aim of the programmes being the development of successful opposition to communist activities and the possibilities of subversion. The study by Barber and Ronning (1966) supported this theory, by showing that most of the educational programmes revolved around possible solutions to communist aggression and techniques of dealing with extremist guerrilla movements.

The dominant element of any such technical assistance is, however, the training of personnel to operate the equipment which DCs export to the Third World; as we have seen, there is a continuous tendency in all nations towards capital-intensive military activity. The appraisal of such assistance should therefore be viewed in the light of the consequences of the import of weaponry.

The annual average importation of major weapons in recent years, in terms of the amount of resources paid out by the LDCs, amounts to around $7000 million and this total represents 3–4 per cent of total LDC imports of all kinds. However, the category of 'major weapons', upon which the above calculation is based, only represents

TABLE 4.4 Burden of Arms Imports, 1975, in $US '000 million. Totals may not add owing to rounding

	Weapons imports (A)	Total imports (B)	$\frac{A}{B}\%$	National income (Y)	$\frac{A}{Y}\%$
Middle East	3.61	39	9.3	158	2.3
South Asia	0.41	10	3.9	109	0.4
Far East	0.65	45	1.4	126	0.5
Africa	1.17	41	2.9	123	1.0
Latin America	0.77	56	1.4	367	0.2
Third World TOTAL	6.61	191	3.5	883	0.7

Source: Data from SIPRI (1977), pp. 306–7; IISS (1977); UN (1976), pp. 424–33.

some 50 per cent of the total import of military 'hardware', with the result that the actual resource commitment is in excess of 6 per cent of total imports. Table 4.4 illustrates this resource commitment for the year 1975 in terms of imports and national income for the main areas of the Third World.

From these data, we observe that a little under one per cent of LDC national income is devoted to the purchase of military equipment from abroad (or a little above one per cent if minor weaponry is included). However, the bulk of these imports are required by a relatively limited number of nations, namely the Middle Eastern countries which have been actively engaged in conflict, North African nations such as Libya which are currently expanding their forces, and South Africa, which is taking counter-revolutionary precautions. In most other cases, we find that the burden of arms imports is considerably lower – only a few aircraft, a submarine or some land vehicles might be imported each year.

If we argue that military imports can be justified in terms of their being an essential requirement for the purpose of waging war, it becomes unrealistic to attempt to isolate the economic implications on the same terms as the domestic defence budget. Imports might be necessary to preserve the very existence of a nation, or to prevent the overthrow of the particular governmental form. On this level of self-preservation, economics ceases to have any true meaning and resource costs, in the abstract, become largely irrelevant to policy decisions. Intuitively, this would appear to be true, up to the point of internal economic collapse. The extreme level which characterises the Middle Eastern nations would appear to be an example of such a necessity.

In other cases, importation might be necessary for strategic reasons even though a war is not actually occurring. This justification could apply to India's imports after independence – they were designed to serve a deterrent function and importation is the only method of obtaining a viable deterrent force in a short space of time.

Although superficially arms imports do not appear to absorb a particularly large quantity of resources, they do carry with them additional, 'hidden' costs. The simple acquisition of the equipment is not the final expenditure as far as the LDC is concerned, as defence material has to be operated and maintained. SIPRI (1971) has made some estimates of such running costs.

Libya, for example, purchased over 200 Mirage fighter aircraft from France, at a cost of some $750,000 per plane. The additional costs will amount to $250 per plane per flying hour for servicing the machines, a task which requires the services of 50 trained personnel per machine for maintenance, overhaul and support. The cost of training such a mechanic has been estimated at $50,000 over three years: clearly, the cost of training the personnel to operate the machines far exceeds the actual cost of the aircraft. Simply maintaining the squadrons in the air for one hour each week will cost Libya several million dollars per year.

The army branch of the services is no less expensive. Total coverage for a company of tanks – maintenance, spares, fuel, back-up facilities, buildings, administration – is likely to cost the LDC concerned around $2 million per annum, in addition to the costs of the tanks themselves. It is the navy, however, which is the most expensive branch – a single destroyer absorbs over $140,000 each year, excluding the very high costs of docking and harbouring.

Finally, Barnaby and Huisken (1975) present a neat illustration of the 'hidden cost' problem:

> ... the F-4 Phantom fighter aircraft has a unit cost of about $5 million including spares and, in the US experience, requires thirty-five maintenance man-hours for every flying hour. To operate a squadron of twenty-four of these aircraft, assuming that each flies fifty hours per month, requires a work-force of nearly 1,000 persons, the bulk of them skilled technicians. (p. 46)

When such figures are taken into account, military imports do not appear to be such an attractive proposition, especially if these operating costs are not to be met under the terms of the provision of assistance. In allowing for such factors as maintenance and the training of personnel, the actual resource commitment for the import of weaponry could easily double the cost in terms of the equipment's purchase price.

When appraising costs, it is import to be able to distinguish between the various elements of assistance, i.e. how much is the LDC actually paying for the arms imports, and to what extent is the purchase subsidised? Aggregate data does not provide sufficient insight, but two significant generalisations may be made.

First, the more important the LDC is to the DC supplier, economically or strategically, then the cheaper will be the costs of assistance to the recipient. The FDAs, for example, receive most of their US assistance as aid, rather than on a market trading basis.

The ultimate example is the case of Vietnam – in 1969, this state received $235 million in arms imports from the USA, although the actual US sales to Vietnam were less than 1 per cent of this figure.[7]

Secondly, there exists a strong correlation between the recipients of military assistance and the recipients of economic aid. This is because economic aid, especially bilateral aid, is generally provided for hegemonic reasons, in parallel with military assistance. Again, in the case of Vietnam, more bilateral aid was sent here by the Western bloc between 1969 and 1971 than to any other Third World country except India. On a per capita basis, this aid allocation was even higher than India's. South Korea accepted $300 million in US aid in 1968 – mostly military assistance – and occupies fifth position in the economic aid 'league table'.

Our analysis therefore suggests two 'ideal types' of assistance costs, relevant to areas which are not importing specifically for the purposes of warfare. On the one hand, assistance costs will be *lowest* if:

(i) the LDC concerned is of strategic or economic importance to the DC concerned, in that there will be a greater element of 'aid' in the transaction, often accompanied by economic aid,
(ii) the assistance is related to the appropriate defence requirements and to the civil economy.

The Indian experience of the mid-1960s serves as an illustration. Between 1962 and 1965, India was considered an important area by the West, owing to its proximity to the Communist nations. Similarly, the USSR was anxious to diminish the Western influence and to develop India as a potential support against China. As we have seen, assistance flowed in, containing a large 'aid' component, and much of it was related to civil development. This military assistance was coupled with economic aid, India receiving the largest individual share of Western development funds.

Conversely, the costs of assistance will be *highest* if:

(i) the LDC is of little strategic or economical value;
(ii) assistance is related to the provision of 'prestige' or advanced weapons with high running costs and few civil linkages.

South Africa provides a clear example of this extreme. The 1963 UN arms embargo was accepted by most of the main arms suppliers with the exception of France, which found itself as a monopoly supplier to a nation with plentiful resources – during the 1960s, France supplied over 50 per cent of South African requirements. France was clearly in a strong position to force up the price of armaments and this high cost was one of the factors which obliged South Africa to begin the development of an indigenous arms industry.

To some extent, high costs are also the case in Latin America. After the Second World War the USA provided aid to the region owing to its strategic importance in the Southern Pacific and Atlantic. However, once hegemony had become established, US assistance began to take two forms – aid for counter-insurgency purposes to protect American investments, and military trade in major weapons. The arms trade can be run as a distinct and economic venture once hegemony has become established via aid and other factors; indeed over 80 per cent of US weapons exports to Latin America between 1962 and 1968 were in the form of direct sales. Given that interstate conflict has been minimal in Latin America for a considerable period, the majority of major weapons in that region serve a 'prestige' function and provide tangible illustrations of the power of the various service branches in the various countries. Naturally, the demand for advanced weapons will impose high costs on the economy, given the costs of maintenance and operation, and the minimal civilian linkages.

The political involvement of the DC supplier, which is intertwined with the provision of assistance, is just one factor which makes the evaluation of the economic costs of assistance particularly difficult. Countries might, for example, find themselves acquiring armaments cheaply in resource terms, although they are also obliged to enter into a military alliance with the provider. Economic gains will, of necessity, be traded-off against the limitations imposed by the terms of the treaty. Again, in some cases, assistance transactions might yield a positive benefit if costs are more than compensated for by a parallel influx of economic aid.

Unlike domestic defence spending, which exists even in peacetime to provide insurance against attack amongst other things, the importation of weaponry usually occurs to meet essential war needs and, in a fight for national survival, the value of sophisticated armaments is considerably enhanced. In other words, a few percentage points of GNP might be seen as a small price to pay for continued existence!

Taking our data from Table 4.4, we might reasonably estimate that the cost of arms imports for the 'average' LDC runs at around 0.5 per cent of GNP, although this figure must depend upon the strategic, economic and political situation of the LDC concerned. This cost is especially significant because it affects an important variable in LDC development – foreign exchange. LDCs have a propensity to demand more imports than they can afford from their export earnings, and the nature of LDC exports – still mainly primary products – does not present an optimistic picture for foreign exchange growth. The purchase of military equipment therefore precludes the possibility of the importation of civil equipment which, were it to be of the investment type, could greatly assist the development effort. If this is the case, the actual opportunity cost of military trade given above could well be an understatement.

If we examine the dynamic aspect of imports, we discover an additional potential hazard. The importation of armaments by one nation can easily lead to a local arms race as each country in the region attempts to gain a strategic superiority. As we have seen, this has been the case in many Third World areas; Argentina/Brazil, Southern Africa and the Middle East. Each nation in the race will constantly increase its import requirements at increasing cost. Furthermore, in order to achieve this superiority, the weapons imported will have to be as advanced as possible, and this will lead to ever-increasing costs of operation and maintenance. For reasons which we shall examine later, once an arms race is begun it is extremely hard to stop, with the result that, by importing some quantity of DC weaponry, an LDC might constrain itself to constant importation to maintain parity with its rivals.

5 Military Regimes

The military regime is no longer the exception amongst the governmental forms of the Third World – it has risen almost to the status of a rule. Indeed, it is virtually impossible to maintain an up-to-date record of military coups. Luttwak (1968) observes that, for the period 1946–67, there were fourteen successful coups in the thirty-five independent African nations – successful in the sense that a military government was established – eight in the twenty-one countries of Asia, fourteen in the twenty-two countries of Latin America, and two in the eight Middle Eastern countries. Since 1967, there has been a progressive escalation in the frequency of intervention; Finer (1975) records forty-one successful coups for the period 1968–75, possibly the most significant being those in Uganda (1971), Chile (1973), Portugal (1974), Chad, Nigeria and Bangladesh (1975).[1] The coup in Thailand (1976) is just one example of an intervention since Finer wrote his paper. Given this increasing prevalence of military governments, it seems pertinent to ask – what is likely to happen to defence expenditure and economic development when the military seizes political power?

EXPENDITURE TRENDS

On the basis of the fundamental assumptions of contemporary economic theory, the idea that the allocation of resources in favour of the military sector must increase after a coup has a certain intuitive appeal. In that men should prefer more economic goods to less, on being given the power to extract more they should naturally do so. As we shall see, this hypothesis can only be accepted with some reservations.

The roots of our analysis are hampered even more than usual by the lack of or the inaccuracy of information. Many of the countries in which coups have occurred possess only the most rudimentary forms of national accounts. In any case, the social upheaval which necessarily follows a coup does not particularly encourage the collection, processing and presentation of data. In situations where the coup heralds the emergence of a major conflict, as in Nigeria after 1966, we should naturally expect expenditure to grow at an

TABLE 5.1 Indices of Defence Expenditure during the Period of a Military Intervention, indicating annual defence spending in the four years preceding, and four years following, a military coup. Expenditure base year equals year of coup equals 100. Data in italics indicate annual defence burden. An asterisk indicates that an additional successful coup occurred in that year also

Country	Year of coup	Years preceding					Years following			
Dominican Republic	1963	125	98	93	97	100	109	103	95	92
		6.1	*4.6*	*4.5*	*3.7*	*3.4*	*3.4*	*3.7*	*3.1*	*2.8*
Ecuador	1963	81	109	109*	107	100	121	139	157	149
		1.9	*2.4*	*2.2*	*2.0*	*1.8*	*1.9*	*1.9*	*1.7*	*1.7*
Brazil	1964	14	18	30	50	100	238	298	532	663
		2.0	*1.7*	*1.7*	*1.6*	*1.7*	*2.5*	*2.2*	*2.9*	*2.6*
Argentina	1966	39*	41	55	67	100	141	125	158	n.a.
		2.2	*2.1*	*1.8*	*1.8*	*1.2*	*2.3*	*1.9*	*1.9*	*1.9*
Ghana	1966	58	44	82	100	100	132	173	197	170
		2.1	*1.8*	*1.6*	*1.6*	*1.7*	*2.6*	*2.8*	*2.3*	*1.9*
Syria	1966	83	n.a.*	110	116	100	116	186	190	195
		n.a.	*7.5*	*7.5*	*7.9*	*6.7*	*5.8*	*10.6*	*10.0*	*11.9*
Iraq	1968	73	81	101	100	100	132	170	171	183
		7.9	*8.8*	*8.5*	*8.4*	*9.2*	*11.4*	*11.2*	*10.3*	*n.a.*
Sudan	1971	70	70	84*	87	100	131	181	183	180
		3.3	*3.4*	*4.1*	*5.2*	*5.5*	*n.a.*	*n.a.*	*n.a.*	*n.a.*
Thailand	1971	47	57	70	80	100	109	114	137	159
		2.4	*2.7*	*2.9*	*3.3*	*3.7*	*3.5*	*2.9*	*2.7*	*2.9*
Uganda	1971	50	71	73	92	100	280	186	n.a.	n.a.
		1.7	*1.9*	*1.9*	*2.0*	*2.0*	*3.6*	*n.a.*	*n.a.*	*n.a.*

Source: UN Statistical Yearbook (Various dates), Tables of Public Finance; SIPRI (1977), Tables 7A; 13, 19, 25, 28, 31.

unprecedented rate owing to the needs of warfare, and this factor serves to cloud any conclusions we might reach regarding 'normal' military demands.

Table 5.1 presents data for ten countries which experienced military coups during the 1960s and early 1970s. These examples are illustrative of a number of possible expenditure growth paths. One aspect which does emerge reasonably clearly from the figure is the need to make a distinction between long- and short-term expenditure trends. By 'short-term' we mean the few years immediately after the coup, during which time the military is primarily engaged in the consolidation of its power. After this initial period, it is obliged to make longer-term plans and policies for the management and progress of the economy.

There is therefore good reason to anticipate a rise in military expenditure immediately after the coup, and Table 5.1 substantiates this in every case. Having assumed power, the military has to accomplish two tasks. The first of these is the establishment of itself as the new ruling force, thereby eliminating the possibility of mass revolt, or of attack from without by a neighbouring power who wishes to seize upon the momentary weakness of its rival. This latter factor was, for example, the spur to China's militarisation after the revolution. The requirements of the expansion policy are the enlargement of the existing armed forces, deployment of troops throughout the country, an increased demand for military equipment, and other factors necessary for a 'show of strength'.

The second, and equally important, objective is to ensure that the military itself remains internally loyal, negating the possibilities of a counter-coup from within. In simplistic terms, the methods for forestalling this eventuality are ideological and pecuniary. On the one hand, the leadership might provide the military corpus with sufficient ideological commitment to believe in the desirability of its assumption of power for the benefit of society. Should this not be the case, and the leadership is unable to legitimise itself, substantial pecuniary benefits will have to accrue to the armed forces in order to prevent discontent and possible rebellion amongst the soldiers. In the case of Indonesia, the views of the leadership were somewhat more explicit than in many cases – an army commander observed:

A hungry people is not so dangerous as a hungry army... So in the first instance, I am more concerned with the welfare of my boys. (Quoted by Polomka, 1971, p. 110)

In extreme cases, it might be necessary for the military elite to undertake a rapid purge of the potentially disruptive elements within the armed forces; this was the situation in Brazil when, eleven days after the coup occurred, 122 officers were formally expelled from the services.

The problems facing the military in the longer term – to be discussed in the next section – are not conducive to high levels of military expenditure, in that the military has now accepted the responsibility for the overall guidance of the economy. Having established its position with a fair degree of security, it will be anxious to restrict military expenditure to a level commensurate with that of minimum 'wastage' from the national resources. The extent to which this will be possible is dependent upon a number of factors. First, if the military's strength is manifestly supreme, there is less obligation to cut expenditure in that the position of the military is unassailable in terms of popular or internal revolt. Secondly, if the country concerned is reasonably affluent, the military budget, which is still marginal in terms of total resources available, will play less part in the determination of the nation's economic future, and it can therefore remain high, or even be increased, without significant detriment to economic development.

Evidence does suggest, however, that, over a longer period, military expenditures will reach a ceiling and might even begin to fall, given no renewal of hostilities. The analysis conducted by Loftus (1968) presents a useful examination of Latin American defence expenditures during the period 1938–65. This time-span covers the Second World War and also 13 out of the 14 coups mentioned by Luttwak. Of Loftus' conclusions, the following are the most significant for our purpose. First, for the twenty countries considered, military expenditures as a proportion of total public expenditures did not appear to be disproportionately higher in Latin America as compared with the rest of the world. Secondly,

There is no doubt that since the war, there has been in Latin America as a whole a persistent *downward* trend in the military's share of the budget. (p. 38, original emphasis).

Finally, in no case was it possible to find a persistent, consistent pattern of increases in expenditure as a result of internal conflicts, i.e. military coups.

Loftus' study was conducted some ten years ago, and a few additional comments must be made to make his conclusions applicable to the present time. Latin America is unusual in having so many military-governed states in close proximity to one another and the inevitable form of political competition between such governments must take the form of increases in weapons procurement and overall military strength. This is certainly the case with the two major rivals, Argentina and Brazil. Individually, these two nations are the highest spenders in the region although, in statistical terms, their defence burdens appear low owing to their relatively high national incomes. In these two countries in particular, defence expenditure rises must be attributed to the militaries' desires to maintain strategic and political dominance, both internally and externally. Furthermore, since the 1973 coup, Chilean military expenditure has followed a similar path for similar reasons. An important, and related, point is that military expansion has been accompanied by the development of indigenous weapons production in these nations, especially in Brazil where several different types of aircraft are currently being manufactured, some intended for export to other LDCs.

The cross-section study undertaken by Terrell (1971) supports Loftus' findings for a wider sample of nations. He develops a model with three variables and these are (i) social stress, measured as 'negative satisfaction' such as low GNP, low levels of calorie intake, absence of basic amenities and so forth, coupled with social cleavages such as the number of ethnic and separationist minorities; (ii) political instability, measured by social turmoil such as riots, demonstrations, civil wars and military coups; (iii) military effort, measured as the proportionate military expenditures weighted by the percentage of the population under arms.

Terrell found a strong relationship between stress and instability, after some threshold level, suggesting that a certain amount of stress has to accumulate before it is manifested as political activity. Of greater importance from the point of view of our study is his conclusion that a slight inverse correlation existed between political instability and military effort, especially amongst the Third World nations.

Patterns of post-coup military expenditure differ widely from nation to nation. Although our evidence suggests that there need be no long-term rise in defence spending after a coup has occurred, it is clear that the trend for individual countries must be a function of the character of the regime in power.

ECONOMIC DEVELOPMENT

The development of the economy under a military government is inevitably bound up with the original reasons for the military's intervention. It is probable, in other words, that the particular cause of the intervention will dictate the subsequent military-directed economic policies. Finer (1962) presents us with a useful taxonomy of the factors involved in the military's involvement in politics.

First, several forces may exist which tend to *inhibit* the armed forces from intervention. Possibly the most important is the acceptance of the principle of 'civil supremacy', the internalised belief on the part of the military that it is its appointed role to be subservient to civil authority. Supporting this principle may be the ethic of professionalism, or expertness, where the armed forces conceive of themselves as holding down a particular traditional occupation within the social system, with the moral obligation to perform this to the best of their abilities. Additional inhibiting factors might be the fear that politicisation might lessen the effectiveness of the armed forces, or that a civil war would result from intervention.

Secondly, we can isolate a class of motives which *enhance* the likelihood of military involvement in politics. At the extreme, the armed forces could possess an almost messianic belief in themselves as the logical rules of the state – Finer cites Salazar of Portugal as a believer in the 'manifest destiny' of soldiers. Another important motive is the belief that the policies of the civil government are not coincident with the 'national interest' and this attitude naturally presupposes some implicit value-judgement on the part of the military as to how the country ought to be governed. This variant is less pathological than the former as, in this case, the military simply sees itself as the repository of rationality at the current time (rather than in perpetuity), in opposition to the civil government's viewpoint. Many military coups are justified in terms of their appeal to the national interest and such governments often promise a return to civil, or quasi-civilian, rule once circumstances permit. As we have seen, an additional motive for intervention is the belief on the part of the military that its sectional or corporate interests are threatened by some particular policy of the civil government.

Finally, the military will not only require a motive to intervene, it will also need the opportunity. Such opportunities are most likely to occur when civil dependence upon the armed forces is higher than usual, such as during periods of international or internal crises – in Thailand in 1976, for example, the coup was presaged by internal unrest and the growing likelihood of communist invasion. Particularly in the case of 'national interest' interventions, the military might also find itself in a position of considerable popularity. The willingness of the mass of the population to actively support the military's involvement would clearly assist the latter's ability to overcome any faith that it might possess in the principle of 'civil sup-remacy'.

Irrespective of the motives for intervention, it seems probable that the economic direction of the nation concerned must react in *some* way with the establishment of a military government, although the nature of this reaction is difficult to specify *ex ante*. A complicating factor is the possibility that *any* type of military coup could potentially bring about the *same* subsequent developments within the economy. For example, a 'national interest' coup might occur if the armed forces believed that the civilian government was not providing a sufficiently high growth rate for the good of the people, whilst a 'sectional interest' coup might also be concerned with accelerating growth, only this time to further its private interests. On the other hand, should an economic decline result after the period of the coup, this could either reflect the neglect of the economy by the new government or, as in the case of Burma, reflect an increasing concern to bring about a transition of the economic structure for the eventual benefit of all concerned. In conclusion, therefore, it would appear that, in itself, post-coup economic performance cannot explain the cause of military intervention.

The economic success of a military government after the assumption of power will, to a great extent, depend upon the quality of management and administrative skills which can be mobilised. In many respects, we should expect the military to serve as an efficient national executive, at least in the short- term; as Janowitz has pointed out, the military is a 'crisis organisation'. A basic skill of the military profession should be the ability to adapt to current circumstances, and such a skill should prove valuable during the disruptions immediately following an intervention. Furthermore, the officer class generally possesses administrative abilities and the system as a whole has a refined organisational structure, especially when compared to other LDC institutions. However, once the short-term problems of political transition have subsided, the demands facing the military will be somewhat different. In order to assess the military's effectiveness in long-term economic management, let us consider a few examples.

During the earlier part of the Nkrumah era in Ghana (1957–66), economic development was characterised by two factors – the domination of foreign capital, especially in the export goods sector, and the very slow expansion of indigenous production. After 1961, Nkrumah attempted to remedy the situation by a massive capital programme along traditional Soviet lines, coupled with the ideal of nationalisation and state-ownership of production. This had the consequence of imposing severe consumption restrictions upon the people of Ghana, and the military also found its allocation stagnating after 1962. Foreign capital became alienated owing to the newly-imposed ownership restrictions. Nkrumah's policies were not helped by the visible extravagance and mal-planning of his projects – the enormous airport in northern Ghana, far in excess of requirements, and the Volta Dam project, whose benefits to Ghana were exceptionally long-term. A swing towards the East for capital and aid was the natural conclusion.

Further antagonised by the preferential treatment accorded to Nkrumah's personal defence forces, the military overthrew the civil government in 1966. The immediate priority of the new leadership was to secure international recognition, a problem faced by all such regimes given the nature of the interactions between their economies and those of the rest of the world. In the case of Ghana, recognition was secured almost immediately, once the West had come to appreciate the army's intentions. Private enterprise was re-established, with the provision of security of investment and the withdrawal of the threat of confiscation, resulting in the rapid influx of aid, capital and credit.

The army's leaders showed themselves remarkably adept at coping with the problems of economic management. In statistical terms, a certain amount of development certainly occurred in post-coup Ghana, and the record was certainly no worse than that of the Nkrumah era. Although growth was slow immediately after 1966, the index of GNP was exhibiting an annual increase of around four per cent per annum by the beginning of the 1970s.[2]

Indonesia's military rulers also met with some success, although the short-term consequence of the military supersession was undoubtedly a polarisation within the elite, between those committed to some form of modernisation and those bent on personal gain from profiteering. This polarisation necessitated a certain degree of political repression during the years following the coup. On the economic front, Suharto succeeded in attracting a considerable amount of resources for the purpose of national reconstruction – $US 1000 million immediately after the coup, over a ten-year period, $US 110 million to develop the copper industry, and $US 175 million for agricultural and construction projects.[3]

Suharto made constant reference to the poor economic conditions inherited by his regime. Inflation had run high – Suharto quoted figures of 650 per cent for 1965 – and the allocation of production factors, as well as the public finances, had been chaotic. In statistical terms, the military regime performed well. Exports in 1969 were nearly double the 1963 figure; in fact, most areas of production yielded higher outputs than the First Development Plan actually advocated – textiles for example showed a 30 per cent increase in the first year. Suharto was eager to add that a significant part of the progress attained could be attributed to infrastructural development, a sector in which the army, acting as a productive force, played an important role. National income data supplements these particular indicators – from an annual growth rate of 1–2 per cent during the five years preceding the coup, post-coup rates had accelerated to over 8 per cent by 1970.[4]

A major problem for the military rulers in Indonesia has stemmed from the fact that, in terms of numbers, the armed forces are extremely large. These forces are a legacy from Sukarno's time, when they were subsidised from available economic reserves. Suharto has attempted to provide a role for his soldiers in the development process, both to enhance Indonesia's development prospects and also to diminish the defence burden on the economy. Indeed, about one-third of the 180,000-strong army is engaged in civil and administrative duties.[5]

Nevertheless, the case of Indonesia does serve to illustrate some of the more positive effects of military intervention. As Polomka (1974) observes:

Indonesia does not provide an example of a military coming to power and spending great sums on arms and propaganda in order to maintain its position. Expenditure in both these fields has been at a far lower level in the post-1966 period than during the Sukarno era. In contrast to the latter's stress on the 'spiritual' aspects of 'nation-building', the Indonesian military has shown itself to be obsessed with a sense of the country's economic and technical backwardness and with a conviction that the state's continued existence depends upon establishing, in political and economic stability, a *sine qua non* for economic development and the establishment of effective institutionalised government. Nor has it excluded civilians from effective power. Civilian technocrats remain dominant in the economic and technical spheres, and to some extent exercise important roles in the broader political realm. The military 'voice' usually only becomes decisive when questions of security are weighed in the balance. (p. 33)

As Ianni (1970) has shown, a number of Finer's intervention factors were present during the 1964 coup in Brazil. First, the military in this country had only a weak adherence to the principle of 'civil supremacy'. Indeed, as coups had previously occurred in 1937, 1945, 1955 and 1961, it might be fairer to say that it was rather a tradition of *military* supremacy that existed. Secondly, although the economy had performed well up to the end of the 1950s, after 1961 a severe depression set in, to the extent that per capita incomes appeared to fall in 1963. The military reacted to this economic decline in both a 'sectional' and a 'national interest' manner. From a selfish point of view, the armed forces found that the growing inflation was eroding their absolute standards of living, and this problem was exacerbated by a narrowing income differential between themselves and what they regarded as being the lower social classes. In addition, and from a national perspective, the leaders of the military were in sympathy with the remainder of the middle classes in believing that the policies being pursued by the existing government were unlikely to bring about any beneficial economic changes.

In fact, as Ianni has shown, the Brazilian economy had come to a crossroads. Initially with the aid of foreign capital (mostly American), Brazil had developed a strong economic base by this time, and the various opinions within the populist democracy were undecided whether to continue this logical advance towards full-scale international capitalism, or whether to use the resource base as a stepping-stone to the attainment of a more socialist state. The military coup can be seen as a pre-emptive action to ensure the acceptance of the former option.

The economic policies of the military regime were directed, first and foremost, towards the integration of Brazil into the world capitalist system. This involved a massive and rapid industrialisation programme, particularly orientated towards the production of high-technology export items. Furthermore, one factor necessary to the attainment of this end was the repression of the labour force. This strategy had an additional benefit of attracting considerable amounts of foreign capital, owing to the perceived stability of the regime and its embracing of the ethics of private enterprise.

As we have intimated, the making of an overall evaluation of the success of military regimes in terms of their contributions to economic development is a highly dubious exercise. So many complex factors exist in the determination of development that the isolation of the contribution of a new form of government is clearly not viable. For example, the Ghanaian economy must be strongly influenced by world cocoa prices, irrespective of the nature of the leadership. This is the essence of Brett's (1975) analysis of the Ugandan economy. He sees the present situation as resulting from the increased pressure of demand for resources which began in the 1960s. Owing to fundamental structural rigidities, there has been no corresponding increases in productivity to meet these demands. Furthermore, this rigidity is so strong as to make the form of government, in particular the Amin regime from 1971, almost irrelevant. Also of significance for our analysis is the fact that we are unable to predict how the civil government's policies would have worked out, had they been allowed to stay in power.

Despite these reservations, Nordlinger (1970) undertook a study to examine the possible effects of military rule on socio-economic development in Third World countries, over the late-1950s/early 1960s period. His sample of 74 'non-Western, non-communist countries' was differentiated into a number of categories, the criterion for division being the 'political strength of the military'. The continuum therefore had extreme points of unrivalled military control and unrivalled civilian government. This political strength index was then related to a number of indicators of socio-economic development, such as the growth of GNP, increases in industrialisation, changes in agricultural productivity, investment rates and the expansion of educational facilities. Of these potential associations, the only one of any statistical significance was the positive correlation between the military's political strength and increases in industrialisation. In other words, a strong military, either as a government itself or as a pressure group on the civilian government, was likely to be a factor in the stimulation of the pace of industrialisation.

To fully explain such relationships, we must take two factors into account. First, the particular interests of the military will be largely determined by its specific class composition, as Nordlinger observes:

> The day has passed when officers were almost exclusively recruited from the aristocracy and the traditional land-owning class. Today military officers are commonly drawn from the middle class, the marginal middle class, small land-holders, and not infrequently from rural and (in Latin America) urban labourers. Where the officers do not originate in the solid middle class they are at one with their fellow officers in having achieved a solid middle class occupational and status rank. As members of the middle class by birth and/or achievement, soldiers in mufti act in accordance with their class interests and identify with its civilian members. (p. 1142)

Accepting this class-interest theory, we may develop the second point – that the economic strategy adopted by military governments will be selected with a view to the benefits or costs which will accrue to the middle classes as a result of policy changes. Nordlinger accordingly re-estimated his relationships, this time taking account of the importance of the middle-class interest group, and was able to interpret his results in terms of the class connection.[6] He discovered that, where the middle classes were well established, the military was more reluctant to press for socio-economic change for fear of redistributing the economic gains already accrued; conversely, in cases where only an embryonic middle class was in existence, the military was likely to be anxious to press for increased industrialisation and education, as the benefits of these largely accrued to its own particular class. As the middle classes grew in size, it should therefore be anticipated that the policies of the military would become progressively conservative.

Finally, Nordlinger also made an inter-regional comparison of development under military influences. In sub-Saharan Africa, for example, it appeared that the military was more committed to development in terms of all the indicators than was its counterpart in Latin America, the relative size and influence of the middle classes being far smaller in the African case.

The data in Table 5.2 indicate the behaviour of sixteen economies from a time-series, rather than cross-section, point of view. The figures do not appear to follow any consistent pattern, although the growth rates do appear to rise after the occurrence of a military intervention, possibly for the reason advanced by Nordlinger or because of more 'national interest' motives – as we have seen, it is extremely difficult to generalise from specific cases.

TABLE 5.2 Annual Total Product Growth, before and after a Coup (% per annum) calculated from GNP data three years before and after the year of the coup

Country	Year of Coup	Pre-coup Growth	Post-coup Growth
Dominican Republic	1963	5.5	0.3
Guatemala	1963	3.8	3.0
Iraq	1963	1.3	8.2
Nicaragua	1963	5.2	5.5
Peru	1963	4.8	4.8
Bolivia	1964	4.0	5.2
Brazil	1964	5.0	3.2
Indonesia	1965	0.8	3.0
Argentina	1966	4.8	5.3
Ghana	1966	1.0	1.8
Sierra Leone	1966	4.0	6.3
Syria	1966	2.3	7.2
Greece	1967	6.9	8.1
Libya	1969	4.4	9.1
Thailand	1971	7.5	6.4
Turkey	1971	6.2	7.1
Uganda	1971	5.0	0.3

Source: UN Statistical Yearbooks (1971) Table 177; (1975), Table 184; (1976), Table 182.

The evidence on the performance of military regimes so far discussed allows us to develop a number of arguments both in favour of and against military regimes as vehicles of economic development.

First, in many cases, the military is the most progressive sector of an LDC economy, in terms of organisational structure, technology and ideology. It therefore possesses an immanent desire for modernisation. On its assumption of power, it is quite likely to press for such a change, if only for the purpose of serving its own ends.

Secondly, a military government is the only governmental form which possesses absolute authority as far as the running of the internal economy is concerned. For this reason, it is in a position to pursue policies for growth which might otherwise have been unworkable, owing to unpopularity or resistance. Thirdly, military governments may give an aura of stability to their countries, making the latter more attractive propositions to foreign investors who provide capital necessary for development. Finally, in those cases where the military accurately reflects the ideological belief structure of its society, it might be able, upon the assumption of power, to cement national unity, with potentially beneficial economic implications.

On the other hand, there are possible disadvantages to the military as a form of government. First, during the period immediately following a coup, evidence suggests that an increase in military expenditure will occur, although this level might well decrease over time owing to the pressures on the economic allocation of scarce resources. As we saw in the previous chapter, the military regime might also favour higher imports of foreign arms for prestige purposes. In that such an increase in defence spending must divert productive resources, this factor could be considered to be detrimental to the development effort, especially if civilian unrest results from the perception of the military as a privileged body. Secondly, the military is often thought of as being too specialist and rigid, with no experience in economic management. Theorists have accordingly argued that military governments must of necessity be transitory. However, evidence suggests – Indonesia and Brazil – that some regimes are more than willing to recruit economic advisers, both from within and from without the country. The very permanence of a number of military regimes attests to their durability.

Finally, military rule carries with it more considerations than those of 'pure' economics. With only a few exceptions, military regimes have tended in the past to adopt an economic framework of traditional capitalism, irrespective of their inheritance from the previous government. This could possibly be due to the fact that many members of LDC military elites receive their training in the Western nations, and these LDCs also obtain substantial military aid from the same source. For example, the US has provided military training to over half of the African nations which have experienced coups. In some cases, it has been suggested that coups and post-coup policies have been engineered by certain DCs but such statements are hard to verify and do not concern us here. Again, the capitalist ethic might be adopted by the regime in order to attract foreign capital, an input which plays an important role in the development plans of many Third World nations, or to serve the military's sectional interests.

Beyond this point, the economist, *qua* economist, cannot go, as the military's commitment to industrialisation and economic growth which we have seen to be possible is in no way a sufficient precondition for 'development' in the widest sense of the term. The absolute power which the military wields permits it to bring about either progress or barbarism with equal ease and, whilst certain regimes have without doubt operated with an overwhelming majority in terms of popular support, many have followed the Acton dictum to become 'corrupted absolutely'.

To counterbalance 'statistical' economic progress, therefore, we must consider the stifling of political dissent and, indeed, the termination of liberties which might well accompany a military takeover. As the economy modernises, the polity becomes progressively more primitive and centrally-directed terrorism replaces socialisation as a means of social control. Economic gains are redirected to ensure the increased well-being of the political, economic and military elite whilst, in most cases, the mass of the population is progressively immiserised. It has been argued that this is the position in the major states of Latin America, which a recent visitor described as

> societies which are not quite totalitarian but are rendered impervious to real democracy: which are not quite colonies but are dominated by foreign capital and technique. And, more irrationally, which are not strategically threatened by any major external foe but which groan under enormously expensive and well-equipped military establishments. If you like, a sort of staging-post between underdevelopment and development, mediated by a quasi-fascist ideology. Fascism without a public works programme for the unemployed. (Hitchens, 1978, p. 38)

6 Military Policy For Development

The preceding chapters of this book have demonstrated that the evaluation of the costs and benefits of defence spending is a complex issue. Several portions of the military budget might, for example, yield civil benefits with the result that estimates of defence expenditure overstate the true economic cost. On the other hand, the purchase price of imported weaponry only tells a partial story in view of the 'hidden' operating costs that are associated with such items. Nevertheless, one fact remains clear – the military sector absorbs resources which might have an alternative use in the civil sector. Because of the net loss in social output which results from the allocation of resources to the military sector, a number of nations have become concerned to discover ways in which the burden of defence might be reduced, and in this chapter we shall consider a number of such methods.

ARMS CONTROL

It is a simple matter to demonstrate that, in a situation where the desires and aspirations of nations are not coterminous, the proliferation of armaments must inevitably continue. Let us consider a hypothetical case of a conflict between the two states of Macaria and Oceana.

At the extreme, a clash of interests between our two countries might precipitate an all-out war, although evidence suggests that this option is very much a last resort of foreign policy in view of the enormous economic and social costs which are imposed upon all parties concerned. A much more common strategy for each of these countries to adopt is deterrence. Under the system of deterrence, each country *threatens* rather than attacks the other – in military erms, this implies that Oceana is given to understand by Macaria hat any interference in the affairs of the latter would result in nilitary retaliation, and vice versa. The vital ingredient of the eterrence mechanism is the fact that the threat can never be borne ut in practice – should one's rival attack, then clearly 'deterrence' id not deter, whilst should one attack first, then one's strategy is learly that of aggression and not of deterrence. The problem which aces both Macaria and Oceana is therefore to maximise deterrence ecause, in such a manner, each nation's freedom of action is also naximised.

The essence of deterrence is credibility. Macaria, in other words, nust make Oceana believe that its will can be forcibly imposed upon hat country should the situation arise. Conversely, Oceana's strategy nust suggest exactly the opposite to Macaria, namely, that it would e Macaria which would be defeated should a conflict actually arise. n terms of conventional strategy, the most effective method of reating credibility is to establish an overt military and strategic uperiority over one's rival; Macaria and Oceana will therefore levote some quantity of national resources to their military sectors in rder to achieve tactical superiority.

We now reach a somewhat paradoxical conclusion. Open warfare learly causes a rise in military expenditures as men and materials re consumed during the conflict. However, conflict via deterrence, a ituation where the whole point of the exercise is *not* to use up the nilitary materials, also appears to necessitate increases in military pending.

Once rival deterrence systems have been established, Macaria and)ceana will be doomed to a perpetual arms race, as we may predict rom a game theory model. Figure 6.1 illustrates a matrix of

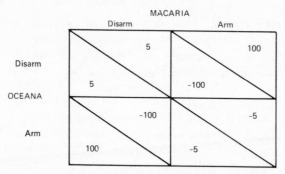

FIG. 6.1   Pay-off Matrix for Two-Nation Armament Strategies

hypothetical 'pay-offs' for our two protagonists, who each face
choice of expanding their defence budgets ('Arm') or of contractin
them ('Disarm'). If both nations were to reduce their militar
spending, it seems reasonable to assert that economic advantage
would accrue to both as the military surplus could now be put t
more socially-productive use in the civil sector. Assuming that o
two states possess similar economic structures, we may evaluate thes
benefits at, say, five units each. At the same time, it may be assume
that neither side has gained any strategic advantage as both defenc
sectors will have been contracted by a similar amount. On the othe
hand, if both nations decided to expand their defence allocatior
there would be a net loss to civil production, and we might represer
this pay-off to each as minus five units. Again, the balance of powe
would be unaffected as both nations have expanded their defensiv
capabilities to a similar extent.

Consider now a case where Macaria escalates its defence spendin
whilst Oceana contracts its allocation. According to the calculus c
defence, this is a recipe for disaster. Oceana's credibility will b
severely diminished as Macaria will perceive a strategic superiority
Macaria's pay-off, in other words, will be extremely high (say 10
units), whilst Oceana's much weakened bargaining position will yiel
an equivalent negative pay-off (-100 units). Clearly, the reverse i
the case if it is Oceana which expands its budget whilst that c
Macaria contracts.

The conclusion of this analysis is that, unless each nation i
virtually certain that the other will disarm, it will be necessary for i
to expand its defence budget. Given that once the deterrenc
credibility is weakened it becomes even more difficult to reconstruc
both Macaria and Oceana are bound to increase their defenc
expenditures.

This model suggests that, in a situation of actual or potentia
conflict, nations acting in isolation will always find it optimal t
increase their defence expenditures. Moreover, the experiences of th
real world do suggest that the deterrence game played by Macari
and Oceana is a fairly accurate representation of reality – consider
for example, the arms races between NATO and WTO, Argentin
and Brazil, South Africa and its northern neighbours, and so forth.

As the earlier chapters of this book have shown, arms racing i
likely to prove a costly pastime, irrespective of any benefits whic
might accrue to the civil sector from that of the military. Even s
although resources will be diverted away from welfare-creatin

:ctors of the economy, such economic costs should not be the sole onsideration. As Kahn (in Brennan, 1961) has shown, a by-product f an arms race is the increased likelihood of war.

In the first instance, the proliferation of weaponry increases the kelihood of unpremeditated war owing to human error or 1echanical failure. This argument is based upon the intuitive law 1at the larger and more sophisticated the mechanism, the greater 1e possibility of breakdown! Secondly, the availability of a larger 1ilitary force will encourage politicians to adopt a strategy which 1ertrand Russell has termed 'Chicken'. In such a game, one 1pponent will make a provoking play in the belief that the other must 1ack down rather than risk an escalation into all-out war – an xample of such a high-risk/high-return strategy was President .ennedy's handling of the Cuban missile crisis in the early 1960s. hould both sides adopt the 'Chicken' strategy, the outcome will 1enerally be fearful, as Taylor (1963) has elegantly demonstrated in 1e case of the First World War:

> Men are reluctant to believe that great events have small causes. Therefore, once the Great War started, they were convinced that it must be the outcome of profound forces. It is hard to discover these when we examine the details. Nowhere was there a conscious determination to provoke a war. Statesmen miscalculated. They used the instruments of bluff and threat which had proved effective on previous occasions. This time, things went wrong. The deterrent on which they relied failed to deter; the statesmen became the prisoners of their own weapons. The great armies, accumulated to provide security and preserve the peace, carried the nations to war by their own weight. (p. 13)

'inally, increases in military strength on the part of a particular ation could mean that warfare becomes an optimal economic trategy for it to pursue, in terms of expected gains and losses. In uch a case, strategic superiority would change a deterrence policy 1to one of aggression and this certainly seems to have been the case f Israel in 1967.

If the proliferation of weaponry brings about economic costs and 1e increased likelihood of war – both generally agreed to be ndesirable – then why have steps not been taken to control arms scalation? As experience evidences, the control of arms is extremely ifficult as a number of factors militate directly against it.

First, protagonists in an arms race will view one another with suspicion engendered by an absence of certainty as to one another's motives, as *The Times*' report of US Senator Edward Kennedy's speech to the Soviet Institute for United States' Studies shows:

'Today, without announcement, the Soviet Government is building new missiles and testing still others'. . . He asked whether this meant preparation for another round of arms competition or whether it was merely due to the momentum of research, without intention to deploy. (20 April 1974, p. 4)

Given the existence of a conflict of interests between rivals, force reduction can never be optimal for one party without almost total certainty of reciprocal action.

When a conflict of interest exists between individuals within a state, an authority (usually the legal system) exists whereby solutions to the conflict may be enforced. However, in the case of nation-states there exists no supranational authority to impose a globally-optimal solution, for nation-states recognise no authority beyond that of themselves. The second problem of controlling arms is therefore that any agreements relating to arms limitation which might be imposed upon protagonists cannot be enforced without recourse to pressure from without. Such a pressure inevitably entails military force, so that the exercise becomes self-defeating.

Thirdly, it would seem that the governments of countries concerned are under no internal political pressure to undertake weapons reductions, as the cross-section survey by Galtung (in Benoit, 1967) indicates. In his analysis of popular opinion in France, Norway and Poland, he discovered that disarmament had not really become a political issue, despite the considerable burden of defence spending in these countries. He believed that these conclusions hold true for most of the nations involved in the East/West 'conflict'. In this respect, it is interesting to note that the major popular anti-aggression movement in recent years, relating to the American presence in Vietnam, was motivated not by a desire for arms limitation but by a reluctance to be involved as a third party in external warfare. In the case of the LDCs, where the political and economic corpus of society is still being moulded, a considerable amount of uncertainty and insecurity must still exist, and these factors equally preclude the possibility of any degree of arms control.

Finally, our 'military-industrial complex' theories suggest that movements towards arms control would be strongly resisted by those groups with a vested interest in the military establishment – military officers, defence industry executives and politicians. 'Complex' theorists argue that the current growth of defence spending arises from the positions of power held by these groups so that, as long as this situation remains unchanged, we should expect no reduction in armaments spending.

Although nations have come together from time to time with the intention of imposing mutual limitations upon defence spending for the good of all concerned, the dispassionate observer does, by and large, have the right to be somewhat cynical as regards the results. The 'superpowers' have achieved a great deal of success in securing limitation agreements over regions of the world which, at the time, appeared to be of absolutely no military significance whatsoever – Antarctica (1959), outer space (1967) and the sea bed (1971). Similarly, biological warfare has been outlawed (1972), primarily because its unpredictability and lack of control make such weaponry unsuitable for offensive or defensive purposes.

On the other hand, the development of militarily important armaments for use in militarily strategic regions has not yet been limited to any significant extent. Rather, the development of a new weapon by country A has generally caused country B to rush to the negotiating table whilst country A tiptoes quietly away. After a while, B's scientists produce an even more horrendous weapon, and the roles become reversed.

The majority of the arms control agreements ratified so far have been those between the USA and the USSR and relate to the possible escalation of nuclear weaponry. Accordingly, Third World nations have not really become involved in either negotiations or in treaties with one another. An exceptional case, however, has been the 1967 nuclear weapon ban in Latin America which has been wholeheartedly accepted by all parties concerned with the exception of the two nations most likely to acquire nuclear weaponry, Argentina and Brazil. In addition, a number of LDCs such as Burma, Egypt, Pakistan, Morocco and Nigeria are members of the UN Conference of the Committee on Disarmament, although this body has been ineffectual in producing any important limitation agreements.

Into this gloomy picture of weapons proliferation we might inject two more optimistic contributions. First, an early concern of theorists looking into the possibility of arms limitation (and at the extreme, complete disarmament) was that the economy would collapse if such an important economic sector were to be contracted. However, it now seems well-established that this need not be the case, even in nations which possess an extraordinarily high defence burden such as the USA. On the basis of his analysis of a United States Arms Control and Disarmament Agency proposal to progressively contract the US defence sector, Suits (in Benoit and Boulding, 1963) concluded that:

> an abrupt... termination of the defence program would unquestionably precipitate a serious economic crisis. But a program of general and complete disarmament..., scheduled over a twelve-year period, combined with only the most elementary offsets in the form of tax reduction and transfer expenditure creates an adjustment problem of a lower order of magnitude than that posed year in and year out by the growth of the labour force and increased productivity. In fact, the impact of disarmament represents a slight – almost unnoticeable – intensification of the problem of adjustment to economic growth in general. (p. 111)

A study of the United Kingdom (EIU, 1963) has suggested similar conclusions and has examined many potential usages for the liberated resources, such as the extension of welfare services and the reduction of the national debt. In nations such as the LDCs, where defence sectors are so much smaller, we should anticipate correspondingly smaller problems in the reorganisation of economic activity under conditions of arms limitation; we may generally conclude that defence contraction is economically feasible.

Secondly, the continued growth of military expenditure has finally brought about a reaction from the militaries themselves, a reaction which has taken two forms. On the one hand, strategists and politicians alike have become concerned that the escalating costs of increasingly-sophisticated weaponry have prevented deployment on a scale which was previously attainable. Technological development in the arms race has, in other words, entailed increasing expense. On the other hand, it has accordingly become vital to assess the efficiency and effectiveness of particular weapons systems out of the many systems which might be currently available. In simple terms, the military has become faced with the question – given X million pounds to spend on a deterrent, should we buy missiles or tanks or ships or other such hardware, or even combinations of all types?

These conditions lead to the development in the early 1960s of a new form of budgeting technique which, it was hoped, would ensure that resource allocation to defence were conducted more economically.

As we saw in Chapter 2, the traditional form of budgeting was an inefficient tool as it classified resource costs according to the type of resource employed as an input. Correspondingly, no regard was paid to the particular use for which the resource was needed. Typically, we saw information classified by service under such headings as remuneration of personnel, purchases of supplies such as petrol and food, construction and research and development. Such data tell us nothing about the ends which are being served, as we are only aware of what goes into the production of defence and not what comes out.

By contrast, present budgeting techniques are orientated towards classifying costs according to the output of defence production, in terms of the functions for which such costs have been incurred. Hartley (1974) regards the following as the key questions to which output budgeting addresses itself: (i) what are the national defence objectives and is it possible to formulate strategic programmes to meet these objectives? (ii) what are the real resource costs of these programmes? (iii) what are the results of expenditure on these programmes? (iv) can the same results be achieved by alternative programmes and what are the associated costs and benefits?

In the British case, the key roles of practical output budgeting are played by long-term and 'element' costings, whereby the total defence budget is broken down into functional categories. The UK identifies around 550 basic elements, as defined by objectives, and these are grouped under twelve major categories such as strategic forces, reserve forces, research, training and so forth. The determination of the final budget allocation therefore becomes a dialogue between the senior military on the one hand and the Treasury and political process on the other, on the basis of estimations of (i) the relative priorities of the functional elements and the costs thereof; (ii) the future long-term commitments of present military programmes and the present costs of past programmes; and (iii) the relative priorities of defence, *vis-à-vis* other public sector and general economic activities. Naturally, output budgeting cannot actually *make* decisions but it does provide the necessary basic materials for the making of *improved* decisions, improved because the expenditure data can be coupled with the weighing of objectives by the relevant decision-makers, who will now become aware of the respective resource costs of a number of possible strategies within a more integrated defence system.

Even so, it is clear that better planning has only made *marginal* improvements in the overall burden of defence and, to some extent, the value of such planning is still debatable. To return to Enthoven's example of Chapter 2 we might conclude that the purchase of additional missiles does not significantly improve the firing-to-kill ratio. The military, on the other hand, might argue that, given the destructive capacity of modern weapons, we should plan to provide as near 100 per cent defensive coverage as possible – anything less could result in substantial destruction of the power in question. In a world where one single missile can destroy a whole city, the role of marginal analysis could be regarded as limited!

Finally, as we saw, the Third World nations do not operate with such a high opportunity cost as do the DCs, implying that even less could be gained from better planning. This does not mean, of course, that the planning process should not be refined as much as possible.

From our observation on arms control, we must conclude that the military sector, *per se*, seems to have established itself on a permanent basis and will therefore always require resources to be diverted from civil productions. However, let us now investigate the possibility of the assumption of a 'dynamic' role by the armed forces, so that they can act as a deliberate agent in the development of its society. Some nations have already appreciated this possibility, and we shall use them as examples of the potential of this policy. Broadly speaking, the military has two alternatives. First, it can direct some of its activities and resources towards non-military activities, such as public works, and, secondly, it can redefine itself as an integral element of civil society. Both of these courses of action still permit the military to retain its strategic functions. The alternatives are not mutually exclusive – rather, they are points on a continuum – but exposition is facilitated by dealing with each individually.

Before leaving these issues of arms control, we might consider one of the most recent contributions to the proliferation debate. Although largely unrelated to the specific problems of the Third World, the report of the UK Labour Party Defence Study Group (LPDSG, 1977) is of general interest as it pays particular attention to our two 'optimistic contributions', namely, the economic viability of armaments reduction and the need for rational planning. A belief in the necessity for weapons reduction has a long history in the UK Labour Party, based upon the notion that the very existence of armaments constitutes a serious threat to world peace and also that military expenditure directs resources away from 'socially desirable' production. These factors played a key part in LPDSG's policy analysis, the main recommendation of which was the reduction of the UK defence burden to a level commensurate with that of European NATO allies by means of the rigorous application of cost-effectiveness analysis of weapons systems. Based upon a substantial volume of empirical data, a variety of resource-saving options were presented (e.g. the running-down of the nuclear submarine fleet, or the air force), these options representing an average saving of some 20 per cent on projected defence budgets. In parallel, studies were also carried out which convinced LPDSG that the necessary adjustments to the economy (to redirect activity away from defence production towards civil manufacturing industry) were entirely feasible.

In many respects, we can regard the LPDSG study as a 'pilot' project for future developments in the way in which we might wish to think about the resource allocation problem in the context of defence. Even so, the reactions to the project on the parts of the Government, the media and the public, which have ranged from casual interest to open hostility, suggest that these beliefs are by no means shared by all at the present time.

CIVIC ACTION

We take the term 'civic action' to describe cases where the military provides deliberate benefits to the civil economy by acting in a 'non-military' manner. Lee's analysis of the post-independence African states (Lee, 1969) gives us a foretaste of this potential role. Lee highlights the close relationship between labour policy and security, in terms of the increasing maldistribution of the population. He argues that the situations of urban unemployment and rural depopulation might find their solutions via the development of a sense of identity and discipline within the society, and the instilling of such a sense is clearly within the military's capabilities.

The most suitable starting-point for discussion, however, is the work of Hanning (1967), entitled *The Peaceful Uses of Military Forces* (PUMF) and it is well worth quoting Hanning's opening paragraph in its entirety, as it serves to set the scene for the subsequent analysis.

The primary purposes of military forces must be recognised as being to provide for the internal and external security of their countries. However, in a world of sizeable standing military forces, the concept of the peaceful use of such forces along constructive lines of benefit to the community at large deserves exploration and definition. Indeed, in many countries, such use is an integral part of attaining national security and not a pure supplement. There are skills required in modern military structures that are capable of being used for non-military purposes, skills that in some areas of the world are in short supply. To be found in military forces are individuals and units skilled in engineering, medicine, communications, transportation, procurement and distribution techniques, and adult training and education. Further, the period of military service provides an opportunity for general education and for training, or the basis for further training upon release, in such skills. (Hanning, 1967, p. xvii)

Let us examine the concept implied by the term 'modern military structures'. Hanning indicates that his notion of the military is that of the professional career-orientated force, whose role, as in most DCs, is primarily related to the maintenance of security. This is reflected in the type of examples he chooses to cite throughout his work. Furthermore, he is concerned with the sort of operations which we have discussed previously, such as education and enterprise, although the context now broadens to include the civil sector. This being so, the roles advocated for PUMF fall into three major categories, namely (i) disaster and emergency relief, including the provision of essential services when those of the civil sector become disrupted; (ii) education and training, including the development of individual self-discipline – training should be integrated with national manpower policy and resettlement programmes; and (iii) economic and social programmes, although the role of the military should be complementary, the civilian effort remaining the primary agent for development.

The reasons advanced for the desirability of PUMF are already familiar to us. They include the issue of the allocation of scarce resources (the classic 'guns versus butter' dichotomy), and also the fact that cuts in military expenditure and manpower seem to be impossible to make, owing to the vested interests of military personnel and the other factors outlined earlier. It is therefore vital for nations to discover ways in which the economic burden of defence might be reduced.

From Hanning's material, it would appear that PUMF could produce two major effects. First, there would be a 'humanisation' of the military via the improvement of its image, to develop a feeling of co-operative effort rather than one of potential oppression, although this must be counterbalanced against the possible hazards of deprofessionalisation. Secondly, PUMF could make a contribution to the development effort owing to the inherent attributes of the military, namely trained labour, technical skills, discipline and specialist knowledge.

The Central Treaty Organisation discussed the operational criteria for PUMF at a conference at Shiraz, Iran, in 1964. Their recommendations give further insight into the workings of such a system.[1] They included the following requirements: (i) the efficiency of military training should not be impaired, in respect of strategic considerations; (ii) the ratio of civil to military participation in projects should be as high as possible; (iii) preference should be given to short-term projects; (iv) the image of the armed forces should be seen to be improved; (v) projects should be initiated by the civil sector. These criteria clearly place PUMF into the first categorial type described above – the redirection of surplus military energy towards civil development. A cynical viewpoint might be to conclude that the whole operation is merely a 'public relations' exercise to increase the military's prestige within the community. Naturally, there is some element of this, but to adopt this attitude completely is to neglect many of the benefits accruing from the use of the PUMF method.

Hanning himself examines these benefits by outlining the practices of some sixteen nations, ten of these being LDCs under our definition. He places heavy emphasis upon the educational and training aspects of the military profession, and his instances serve to substantiate many of the points made earlier. For example, Peru and Iran have been aiming at the production of soldiers of sufficient educational standards to provide instructional foci upon demobilisation and return to civilian life. The types of specialisation are diverse and depend upon the country concerned – they range from elementary academic competence, through business training, to agriculture and public health.

Of particular interest is the role of the military in civil engineering projects. Hanning considered, for example, the case of road construction through a forest region in Peru and construction estimates revealed that capital-intensive jobs, such as excavation and the building of the foundations, cost approximately the same amount whether being undertaken by the military or civilian contracters. However, labour-intensive activities were much less costly when being undertaken by military labour – in the extreme case of pipe-laying, the military cost estimates were at around 3 per cent of the civilian figures. Such a low estimate is naturally due to the fact that military labour can be considered as costless – wages would have to be paid in any case, irrespective of the tasks performed.

A further example was the construction of the Gilgit road in Pakistan. In 1956, the Public Works Department estimated the construction costs of the road at 60.5 million rupees. However, when it was decided to entrust the project to teams from the armed forces, the estimated costs fell by 50 per cent, thus liberating resources for alternative uses.

A corollary of the cheapness of military labour is the unfortunate possibility that this could be a direct cause of civilian unemployment. Clearly, a government must bear this fact in mind when deciding upon the possibility of using the armed forces in a construction project. Nevertheless, the possibilities remain that, first, the cheapness of military labour might be an important factor in making a project economically viable, possibly entailing the use of complementary civilian labour, and, secondly, resources might be liberated for use in other employment-generating projects.

The Indonesian experience provides a useful example of the transition towards a civic action policy, where benefits occur deliberately rather than coincidentally. The military coup of 1966 was a reaction to Sukarno's regime, which had been characterised by economic decline and political tensions. The army had become frustrated by the limitations of civilian rule, which did not allow sufficient scope for the prevailing military ideology of modernisation. The new regime therefore established itself on a platform of stabilisation and 'modernisasi' – economic development and the strengthening of national unity. As we have seen, this policy has met with some success.

The army's role in development was partly determined by ideological considerations and partly by practical necessity. At the time of the coup, the Indonesian military was extremely large and had adopted the aloof, professional orientation. It came to be appreciated that, with little to do after the conflict, the soldiers could easily become discontented, and so a programme of public works was launched, of the standard road-building/ditch-digging type.

The Indonesian military also regarded itself as the spearhead of change, with the conclusion that it must adopt an overt national-leadership role.

> We cannot have welfare state by sitting on our bottoms. We have to work and sweat. This is understood by my boys... We have to give an example... We cannot say 'Let's improve production' and do nothing ourselves. People see us and say the army is not so bad if they see us doing things that are productive. (Indonesian army commander, quoted by Polomka, 1971, p. 111)

In all fairness, it must be admitted that a major proportion of the initial programme was orientated towards the improvement of the welfare of the military. The army commander quoted above also mentioned the army family rehousing programme, his own command having erected one thousand such homes. Even so, he conceded that such preferential activity was becoming rarer, as progressively more of the army's efforts were directed towards the civilian sector; the Minister of Trade 'is squeezing us'. As we saw, the initial favouritism towards the military was politic – the leadership of the armed forces was attempting to cement group loyalty before aiming at a development policy which ran the risk of alienating military sub-sectors.

Civic action techniques exist, in some form or another, in many nations, and the potential clearly exists for them to be even more widely applied. Naturally, the degree of sophistication varies between countries. DCs, for example, are able to establish advanced facilities to provide their soldiers with a level of training commensurate with that obtainable in the civilian sectors. LDCs, on the other hand, might only be able to offer the most rudimentary aspects of general education.

We therefore see that a simple extension of military activity can yield benefits to the civil economy, although the armed forces can still maintain their primary strategic function. The policy merely requires a slight departure from the established practice, such that the effects become deliberate and planned rather than coincidental. LDCs, therefore, could profitably include the potential contribution of the armed forces into their development plans, to assist civil production in the appropriate area.

The civic action model presupposes the discrete existences of both the military and civil society and the potential interrelationships do nothing to destroy the defining characteristics of each. However, our second option – the redefinition of national service and the role of the military – entails a far greater degree of actual integration and merger between the armed forces and their parent societies. It therefore differs from civic action in both degree and kind – it is civic action and more.

MILITARY AND SOCIAL INTEGRATION

The theory relating to military integration is considerably harder to specify than in the case of civic action. It will therefore be necessary to survey the experiences of a number of nations where forms of integration have occurred, or where it is occurring at present. Subsequently, we may distil generalisations from this evidence.

We have already observed that pre-coup Burma gave scope for some element of entrepreneurial activity on the part of the armed forces. However, after 1962, a much more concrete pattern was established. Lissak (1964) observes that the Burmese military became considerably more production-orientated during the period immediately after the coup, and the general framework of his analysis runs as follows: the key to the process of economic development is the mobilisation of resources, manifested in terms of (i) the development of manpower, (ii) the efficient employment of material resources in the production process, (iii) the transitions in norms and values towards the ideology of modernisation. Burma was successful in attaining a state of mobilisation, owing to the emergence of a military elite well versed in entrepreneurial activity.

The structure of the Burmese armed forces was particularly critical to the success of the integration policy. Firstly, attempts had been made, dating from as early as 1945, to eliminate the non-Burmese elements of the military. Periods of compulsory national service were prescribed for both men and women, including members of those sections of the population normally excluded from military service, such as doctors, teachers and engineers. Because of the high input of short-term soldiers, the likelihood of military training permeating through to the civil sector was enhanced.

The reasons for the economic consciousness of the army hinge upon the economic crisis of the late 1950s. Output appeared to be falling, labour was in short supply, national unity was threatened and the cultural identity was becoming confused. These factors led the military to redefine its role in society which in turn necessitated, as far as it itself was concerned, the assumption of political power. Because of this new role, the internal ideological redefinition of the military also became vital. Central to the army's reformed belief-structure was the idea that economic development, defined as the attainment of a socialist economic system, was only possible under a disciplined regime whose authority and power were beyond question.

In practical terms, the military directed its efforts for the attainment of this goal through the media of education and enterprise; indeed it rapidly became the largest business interest in Burma. Its activities ranged across a wide spectrum of the economy – construction, shipping, banking – and it came to own many smaller, individual firms – hotels, shops and garages.

> In developing this large economic complex, the military were opportunistic. Scott & Co., a private English banking firm, had run afoul of the foreign exchange regulations and had had its license revoked. The military seized this opportunity to buy out the enterprise. Rowe & Co., a long-established English firm which had operated Rangoon's largest department store, was facing bankruptcy because for a long time it had been unable to obtain an adequate volume of import licenses. This firm, too, was looking for a purchaser, and the army moved in swiftly. (Walinsky, 1962, p. 261).

After the coup, many officers found their way into civilian posts. This was partly a result of military policy to increase army control, and there was also the desire to utilise the specialist techniques of the administrative officer class. Another factor in the replacement of manpower was the periodic 'purges' for ideological reasons. In its own terms, Burma had some success in its economic venture, indicating that much of military involvement has paid off:

> The Ne Win regime left its mark on virtually every sector of the economy. For the most part, its achievements were constructive. (ibid., p. 263)

It should be pointed out, however, that a major structural transition of the economic system must inevitably bear costs, and Burma's growth in national output was very low at the time and has continued in the same way up until the present.

The experience of Burma might be considered a little extreme for our purposes, in that few nations find themselves under socialist regimes which voluntarily give way to civil government within two years of intervention. However, the example does serve to demonstrate the importance of military-civil integration, which in this case may be summarised as follows: the military appears to represent the paramount agent in the process of mobilisation in LDCs, and it therefore demands essential linkages with the civil economy. If these are not forthcoming, it will be necessary for the military to establish them itself, as it did in pre-coup Burma with the Defence Services Institute. We may therefore deduce that it is inherent in the nature of the military sector to demand some form of integration. One view of the Burmese coup might be to conclude that the then-existing political elite did not take sufficient account of this factor in its management of the economy. At a general level, the parallel between the Burmese experience and that of Uganda is clear – it revolved around the frustration of vested interests.

Our subsequent examples are possibly more representative than the Burmese case and they therefore provide more insights for policy proposals. The first case to be considered is that of China.

For the Western observer, China presents a myriad of problems. Data have not been forthcoming and those which are actually available are subject to a wide variation of interpretation. There also exists a degree of cultural ethnocentricity on the part of Western social scientists, who tend to approach the evidence in ways which are familiar so that, should such evidence fail to fit into the preconceived pattern, it might well be overlooked or accorded only diminished significance. In many ways, China is the least 'Western' country in the world.

It is most important to bear in mind that military integration was bound to be a long-term outcome in China, given the nature of Maoist political theory. This is because a central feature (if not *the* central feature) of Maoism has been the concept of service to society, as Joan Robinson explains:

The Thought teaches us that we must serve the people wholeheartedly, without calculation of loss or gain; that we must be on guard against the sophistries of disguised self-interest. It teaches that problems can be solved; to solve a problem it is necessary to analyse it correctly; mistakes may be examined so as to draw lessons from them; failure must be met with fresh determination. Problems must be discussed with others and mutual criticisms frankly accepted, whether the problem is terracing an eroded gully, setting up a political organisation or rooting out false conceptions from one's own mind. (Robinson, 1970, p. 29)

Coupled with this general principle of service is the realisation that *all* forms of service are equally valuable in moral, if not economic, terms and this implies an essential unity between all occupational groups, soldiers, workers and peasants. China therefore represents an instance of integration precipitated by ideology.

In common with many LDC armed forces, the origins of the present Chinese military stem from anti-colonial and revolutionary activities. In its initial stages, the People's Liberation Army (PLA) existed as an irregular guerilla force with the specific aim of defeating the Nationalist forces, an aim eventually accomplished in 1949.

After the Communist victory, the PLA needed to take on a new function as all its initial battles had been won. As far as China was concerned, the natural example to follow was that of the USSR, where a revolutionary Soviet army had been transformed into a regular and professional force for self-defence. In 1950, a China/USSR alliance was established, the Chinese forces were organised into formal ranks and specialist services, and they were supplied with Soviet military equipment. In addition, military assistance took the form of defence industry construction – by 1953, over 140 Soviet-inspired defence plants were either promised or were in actual operation in mainland China.[2] In the light of such policies, the 1954 Chinese constitution gives us a clear picture of the perceived role of the PLA at that time:

The armed forces of the People's Republic of China belong to the people; their duty is to safeguard the gains of the people's revolution and the achievements of national construction, and to defend the sovereignty, territorial integrity and security of the country. (Quoted by Yuan-Li, 1973, p. 802).

By the end of the 1950s, however, the role of the PLA had fundamentally altered for two major reasons. First, on the political side, it had become apparent that the USSR would only offer reluctant support for China in its relationships with the Nationalists who currently inhabited the off-shore islands, in spite of the formal alliance between the two nations. The USSR was also displaying manifest desires to control Chinese domestic and foreign policy, in order to bring it into line with its own requirements. Secondly, Chairman Mao in particular was becoming increasingly worried by the economic burden which a Soviet-type, professional army was imposing on China and this worry was exacerbated by the slow progress in economic development which was then being made. Furthermore, attempts to limit the armed forces' budget or to involve them in public projects were being resisted by the military leadership.

What, then, has been the subsequent role for the Chinese military forces? In this respect, it is possible to detect three significant redirections of emphasis after the late-1950s.

First, China came to appreciate that, in order to effectively compete in the world as a 'superpower', it must continue to develop its nuclear capability. Although nuclear technology was first introduced into China by the Soviet assistance programme, it soon became clear that complete political and strategic independence could only be achieved if China was capable of constructing its own deterrence forces internally. Accordingly, heavy investment has been undertaken in the nuclear field, a result of which has been the progressive weakening of the PLA in terms of conventional weapons capabilities.

Secondly, the PLA has been required to reverse the professionalisation process of the early 1950s and to adopt a more political and public role – by such means, its economic burden has been reduced and its loyalty to civil society has been enhanced.

> The army's work in this field ranged from agricultural production, water conservation and flood control to industrial production and management. Such activity reached a peak during the Great Leap Forward period when, according to Chinese sources, the army contributed respectively 59, 44 and 46 million man-days of labour to the economy in the years 1958–60. (Baylis *et al.*, 1975, p. 250)

Coupled with the simple factor of increasing labour inputs, there has been an extension of the soldiers's role towards that of political teacher amongst the populace amongst which he or she is working.

Finally, the defence of China has no longer become the sole responsibility of the PLA; rather, the formal armed forces now serve as the vanguard of the militia and it is here that the integration role comes to the forefront. The ideology of China sees the social role of worker, peasant and soldier as inexorably interlinked. There consequently exists a relatively small regular army, composed of regional standing divisions and a number of field divisions 'on alert'. Together, these only draft some 10 per cent of the eligible males each year. However, the remainder of the population constitutes a militia or military reserve, and operates under the auspices of the local standing army. The difference between the two seems to be of degree.

> By 1959 220 million men and women were reportedly members of the militia... Now it was not only supposed to include every able-bodied person, but its role in the defence of China, and in production, were greatly extended as well. The aim of the movement, in short, was nothing less than the militarisation of society. (Ellis and Joffre in Yuan-Hi, 1973, p. 268)

The most recent estimates of the strength of the Chinese forces suggest that the formal armed services are composed of some four million men. The militia itself appears to be subdivided into the immediate military reserves (seven million), the 'ordinary' militia (up to 100 million) and the 'Civilian Production and Construction Corps' (four million).[3] One must add that the aim of the militia movement is not only the militar-isation of society, but also the socialisation of the military.

The militia has become vital to China's strategic outlook with the acceptance of the concept of 'People's War'. Put quite simply, this attitude suggests that, if everyone in the society is a potential soldier, then conquest from without is impossible without annihilation of the entire population. Given a Chinese population of nearly 1000 million, this is clearly a tall order. Clearly, 'People's War' is a logical extension of revolutionary guerrilla activity where irregular forces rely for their success upon the passive assistance of the civil population, in the form of provision of supplies, maintenance of secrecy and so forth. At this new extreme, passive assistance becomes active involvement. 'People's War' is therefore essentially a system of deterrence by defence, designed to advertise the futility of invasion attempts from without, and the nuclear ballistic missile programme complements this defensive posture by suggesting the existence of an attack capability.

Turning away from the purely strategic functions of defence, a major benefit of militarisation is undoubtedly education and indoctrination in the value-neutral sense. This is how the Chinese democratic republic is avowedly being achieved. Military training is the cornerstone of the educational process, in teaching not only the 'standard' subjects and their relevance to everyday economic life, but also discipline and political commitment to induce ideological remoulding. For such a training, all aspects of economic existence may be approached more successfully, at least in terms of the Chinese development ideals. The leading role played by the army and the militia as agents of social change during the Cultural Revolution of the late 1960s attests to the strength of purpose which has been instilled.

Because of the general militarisation process, each commune in China has at its disposal a 'land army' which can operate in the conventional productive manner – digging ditches, building roads and dams and so on. Expenditure on the military is therefore necessarily directed towards real economic production. In particular this policy is important within the PLA itself as it undertakes agricultural projects for its own purposes – in response to the dictum that armies march on their stomachs, we might note that the major part of the Chinese soldiers' provisions is provided by the soldiers themselves.

The Chinese policy on military expenditure therefore falls into two sections. On the one hand, resources have been allocated for all-embracing, maximum efficiency nuclear production whilst, on the other, expenditure has been directed towards development-orientated military activities. The economic policy of China, in which militarisation plays a leading role, seems to have been quite successful – Yeh has estimated a 4 per cent annual growth of net domestic product during the mid-1960s, and the agricultural and industrial indicators have risen accordingly.[4] Possibly such statistical estimates are meaningless, however, in that they are too narrowly defined to genuinely reflect the Chinese attitude to socio-economic development.

Finally, it might be argued that China does not serve as a valid example for our purposes, in that it does not possess a standing army in the sense defined at the outset of this study. However, the process of militarisation transcends the existence of a standing army, and the instance of China merely illustrates the logical consequence of the integration process.

Integration in Tanzania, although based upon similar principles, has not been developed to such a great extent as in China. It therefore provides us with one of the few examples of the integration process as it actually occurs.

In common with a number of other African states, the military forces of Tanzania were a colonial legacy, although they were not, in this particular case, instrumental in the liberation struggle. This factor necessitated a rethinking of the future role. Indeed, the abolition of the military was at one point considered but, for reasons already examined, this alternative has not so far proved feasible for *any* nation. The general state of anomie permeated into the armed forces themselves, manifesting itself as a power struggle between the military and the civilian government. We have already examined the circumstances of the Ugandan military revolt, and it is from this time, when a similar revolt occurred in Tanzania, that the rationale for an integrated military stems.

The army's demands in Tanzania during the revolt of January 1964 were almost identical to those in the Ugandan case, rapid Africanisation and pay increases – 105 shillings per month to 260 – being the most predominant. The military were eventually pacified by some ground being given on both sides (and by some British intervention), but the incident brought the whole issue of the military's purpose to priority level. Nyerere observed:

> The King's African Rifles never taught the men to become soldiers of Kenya, Tanganyika and Uganda. They were just battalions with British officers. So what did we do when we took over? We changed the uniforms a bit, we commissioned a few Africans, but at the top they were still solidly British. . . When I suggested, 'Here are these able-bodied men, why can't they help build bridges', the officers answered. . . 'These are soldiers!' (quoted by Smith, 1973, pp. 119–20)

Eventually Nyerere came to find his ideal:

> an army that understands the problems of building a nation, not an army isolated from the people. (ibid., p. 120)

The policy adopted was therefore one of gradual integration of the armed forces into the social corpus. In the first instance, integration proceeded at a slow pace and a low priority was accorded to the armed forces in the First Five-Year Development Plan (1964–9). However, the Second Plan (1969–74) indicated a significant acceleration. In parallel with the Chinese case, there was an increased orientation towards a form of militia – the National Service – and away from the conventional armed forces, although the two elements were still clearly interlinked. National Service was now to be undertaken by all those receiving secondary or higher education. What was its role?

> The National Service is, in fact, basically not a military force at all; its job is to make a contribution to the development of our economy, at the same time as it provides education in politics and skills for its

members, and inculcates a sense of discipline which they will carry into their post-Service life. It therefore runs farms, builds roads, and does many other productive activities in the country as they are needed (Nyerere, 1971, p. 64)

As the Second Plan attests, more than seven times as many people passed through the National Service than under the provisions of the First Plan. New training schools were constructed and as the Plan states:

> special emphasis will be given in creating productive enterprises in accordance with national priorities. . . this implies an addition to the regular schools and training institutes. It will provide the national economy with an extra push. (MEADP, 1969, p. 62)

It is this policy which, to a great extent, accounted for the rapid growth in military manpower which Tanzania experienced during the late 1960s/early 1970s.

Although different in many respects from Maoist political thinking, the ideology of Nyerere has also implied the long-term inevitability of military integration. In the Tanzanian case, the central political ethic has been referred to as 'communitisation', a philosophy which seeks to combine the best features of traditional African culture with the modern socio-economic environment. As in the Chinese case, mutual assistance and equality are stressed.

The evolution of ideology in Tanzania has provided Nellis (1972) with the basis of a model which demonstrates the importance of such a development within an LDC, and we may use this model to demonstrate an important relationship between ideology and military integration.

Taking Nellis' theory in its most simple form, we first assume that socio-economic policies are implemented and imposed upon the citizens by a ruling regime. This citizenry may be categorised into two groups, the 'politically aware' and the 'politically unaware', the former group being defined as those people who *perceive* the exact nature of the relationship between their particular level of well-being and the policies of the regime. In addition, each citizen may be either 'contented' or 'frustrated', that is, his or her level of well-being may be consistent with his or her subjectively-assessed needs, or else he or she may not be satisfied by the regime's present or anticipated policies. Given this set of axioms, how does the regime implement policies?

In the case of 'unaware' citizens, it seems unlikely that any threat to the stability of the regime will exist, as this group will not relate its fortunes to the regime's activities. In addition, the 'contented' group will naturally have no cause for concern. The success of policy implementation will accordingly be contingent upon the degree to which the regime can 'content' the 'frustrated politically aware'.

The interests of this group will vary with circumstances. Nellis' study, for example, discusses the Village Settlement programme in Tanzania which was designed to 'communitise' agriculture and which necessitated major upheavals amongst the peasantry with resulting discontent. We can, however, discover other such 'frustrated' groups in other countries, such as the landowners and industrialists in Allende's Chile or international corporations in those nations where foreign enterprises have been nationalised.

The threat posed by the 'frustrated' group will be determined by the potential power of that group to precipitate the downfall of the regime. On the one hand, therefore, a policy which frustrates the interests of, say, a pacifist religious minority is unlikely to discover any serious obstacles during its implementation. Alternatively, the greatest threat to the regime is that group with the effective monopoly of the means of violence, the military.

Should the regime therefore find that, in any particular instance, it is the armed forces which it is obliged to content, it is broadly faced with two alternatives. First, it can content them by increasing their material well-being or, secondly, it might content them by imposing on them an ideology, that is, a set of political values, which justifies the particular programme in question. Frustration becomes contentment, in other words, by the provision of resources to meet demands or by the demonstration that the demand themselves are unjustified. In the particular case of a 'politically aware' military, therefore, the risks of intervention or coup may be minimised by either 'bribing' the military into agreement or, by means of ideological remoulding, no longer permitting the military to possess a private interest. However, because bribery still permits the armed forces to retain their private interests, the threat of intervention is simply postponed rather than eliminated as in the case of integration. Subsequent military takeover is accordingly still possible and, indeed, likely, as we have seen in a number of instances.

We have now outlined three examples of military integration. In the case of Burma, integration was more or less forced upon the country, owing to the military takeover. On the other hand, China and Tanzania demonstrate that integration might come about by the deliberate policy of the civil government. By way of summarising our analysis of the whole field of military policy for development, we might ask – why is integration, on any scale and of any type, desirable?

The following reasons in favour of integration may be advanced. First, the armed forces in an LDC represent a heavy resource commitment. In an attempt to maximise the output from this existing input – determined primarily by strategic considerations – it is desirable for the military to engage in some form of productive activity. Secondly, because the military possess certain attributes – organisation, discipline, education, specialist knowledge and equipment – it would seem good policy to use these facilities to benefit the entire population and economy. Thirdly, and given that LDCs tend to be disorientated owing to their rapid transitions from traditional to modern societies, and that the leaders of such countries occupy precarious positions of power, the integration of the military into the wider society will minimise the possibility of social conflict and disintegration. Fourthly, where there exists an ideological weakness within the society, militarisation of the National Service type can assist in the cementing of the civic culture. This particular argument has an illustrious pedigree, having been previously advanced in 1810 by the German philosopher, Hegel:

> . . . when military training was being introduced into the highest form of the Gymnasium, Hegel extols this introduction of a citizens' army which, he points out, has always been, ever since the Greek polis, at the root of the popular identification with the political structure; a standing, professional army, on the other hand, usually goes hand in hand with a growing estrangement between the government and its citizens. (Avineri, 1972, pp. 68–9)

Finally, unemployment, both of school-leavers and of labour in general, is possibly the most pressing problem facing the Third World, especially in view of its cumulative nature. Industrilisation has failed to provide any solution to this surplus, owing to its increasing capitalisation and the limits of the market. Agriculture provides the key to the economy, both in terms of subsistence and exports, but labour is given no incentive to operate in this area. The answer must be seen in terms of an organisation under government control which can initiate and support labour-intensive projects, in the agricultural or infrastructural sectors. The military, or para-military, system provides an excellent starting-point for the development of such an organisation, as the experience of Tanzania suggests.

What evidence exists to support our hypothesis that integration is desirable? In terms of concrete data, the short answer is – very little. Any integration of any consequence has only occurred within LDCs which, in general, possess few forms of economic data. Tanzania, for example, possessed virtually no economic statistics before independence, and sufficient data for macro-planning has only recently become available. As is the case in other countries, Tanzania is still in a state of transition, with the result that the economic effects will hardly become apparent, let alone measurable, for many years to come. Suffice it to say, that for those countries where data does exist, national incomes appear to be rising, albeit slowly. At an intuitive level, some credit must be given to the policy of military and social integration.

At the micro-level, the education, discipline and training functions of the military service – the investment in human capital – will produce economic benefits, the magnitudes of which are more familiar to us. It is generally accepted that the growth rates of economies can only partially be explained in terms of increased inputs and improvements in productivity. Often the cause of over 50 per cent of the rate is left unexplained. This residual factor can be interpreted in terms of increased, but unmeasurable, output caused by education, experience and motivation. In that the very concept of military integration entails these effects upon manpower, increasing outputs are to be expected as a result.

This chapter has been concerned with attempting to discover ways in which the economic burden of defence might be minimised. Given the state of world insecurity and the inherent tendency of arms races to be self-sustaining, we must conclude that arms control has little likelihood of succeeding in bringing about a significant reduction in the resource allocation to defence. The answer, if such an answer exists at all, must therefore lie with civic action and military integration.

There are signs that, amongst those nations with well-established armed forces, civic action policies are becoming more popular – even DCs have come to anticipate the benefits which might accrue, both in political and economic terms. In recent years, for example, the British government has shown an increasing willingness to employ the armed forces in civil tasks whenever industrial disputes have threatened essential services.

Integration, on the other hand, is a different matter. Just as the armed forces can be radical in their attitudes to social modernisation, so they can be equally conservative in their reactions to any attempts to undermine their privileges or to introduce a degree of deprofessionalisation, and this factor will continue to pose problems for Third World countries. As many LDC governments have found to their cost, a non-integrated military can easily become a class military and, in cases where there exists no established principle of civil supremacy or integrationist ideology, unfavourable policies will result in military intervention. The problem is exacerbated by time – the longer the military tradition of independence, then the harder the imposition of integration becomes. At the same time, integration becomes more important as the self-interest of the armed forces consolidates. We might compare this situation to that of a time-bomb which becomes progressively more difficult to defuse as the moment of detonation approaches.

7 Conclusions

The central thesis of this book has been that both domestic defence spending and international military assistance represent a net economic cost to the Third World, in spite of the variety of potential benefits which might accrue as a result of related industrial and manpower developments. It was subsequently argued that, in general, LDCs might reduce this cost by following the example of a number of their company and adopt policies of civic action or socio-military integration. This latter variant in particular appears to supplement economic gains with the political benefit of maintaining civil control over the armed forces to minimise the risk of intervention.

As yet, however, we have not succeeded in proving our result completely, for such a strategy will only economise on resources in our terms if it can be shown that the effectiveness of the military is relatively unimpaired by the implementation of civic action or integration policies. In other words, resource savings of X units must not be accompanied by a fall in the quantity of 'defence' available by more than this amount, or else the new strategy must be deemed inferior to that of the *status quo*. A solution to this final problem necessitates a circuitous route.

How much should a nation spend on defence? This very simple, but fundamental, question has a complex answer. It might be argued by the cynic that the only assessment possible is the retrospective one – nations that lose wars do not spend enough – although this is hardly helpful from the policy point of view! In 1976, the UK Secretary of State for Defence, in highlighting the trade-off which exists between defence and other varieties of social policies, argued that:

> Just as it would be wrong to endanger national security in our concern for social justice, so it is no good having a defence policy which could bankrupt the society it is designed to defend. (LPDSG, 1977, p. 9)

This recognition of the economic issues involved is also clear from Weidenbaum's proposals regarding future US military policy:

> ... I do not advocate funding every new weapon requested by the military. That course of action would quickly lead the nation to military budgets on the order of $100 billion a year, if not more; yet this is hardly a plea for the wholesale slashing recommended by those who urge a $50 billion annual level of defence outlay. The middle ground of $70–$80 billion a year necessary to maintain current levels of preparedness does not represent exactly a penurious attitude. (Weidenbaum, 1974, p. 179)

In a very real sense, however, our initial question and these two observations have thrown us off the scent. We have fallen into the trap of mistaking inputs for outputs and our question should have been phrased thus – how much 'defence' should a nation purchase? It is important to make this distinction because defence expenditure is not an end in itself but simply forms a major ingredient of, or input into, a process which produces as its output 'defence', in the same way that the expenditure on iron ore can be regarded as an input to the production of any particular value of steel output. The output of 'defence' is clearly the more abstract, however, as we have already seen that armed forces may be required to play a number of roles. Even so, we may fairly take the military's primary task to be the maintenance of 'security', the defence of the nation from internal and external threat and the potential to successfully attack others.

In the theoretical world of the neo-classical economic model with fixed prices and constant returns to scale, and X-fold increase in the expenditure on iron ore would yield an equivalent increase in the value of steel output, all other things remaining equal. The input of iron ore, in other words, effectively represents the output of steel. In the case of defence, however, can we be sure that such a principle still applies, for it is only if it does that our two questions amount to the same thing? Indeed, there are several reasons for believing that expenditure and security might be unrelated, that is, for believing that 'more' does not necessarily mean 'better'. We shall return to our Macaria/Oceana conflict to provide some simple illustrations.

First, consider the case where Oceana and Macaria are economically and socially identical except in a few important respects. Macaria happens to have been endowed with plentiful supplies of iron and steel, cheap fuel and a labour force which is content to receive low wages. Conversely, Oceana's material inputs are all high-priced and this implies that, for each tank that Oceana produces, Macaria can construct, say, five at the same total cost. Other things being equal, and assuming for the moment that all wars take the form of tank battles, we should suppose that five tanks could provide a better 'defence' than one and we must conclude that expenditure is unrelated to security in this sense unless relative prices and returns to scale are identical.

Secondly, consider the case where Macaria and Oceana each produce one tank at the same cost, but that of Macaria is technically more sophisticated owing to the innovations and skills of the Macarian military engineers. Again, with other things remaining equal, we should suppose that a fast tank with a two-mile range provides more 'defence' than a slow tank with a one-mile range.

In these two examples, it was assumed that the form of warfare was predetermined. In particular, we stated that all conflicts would be resolved, and hence the level of 'defence' would be tested, over terrain suitable for tank battles. Consider now a situation where Macaria possesses its tank and Oceana equips a dozen men with hand-grenades at far less cost. If we were to continue to fight on our tank battlefield, we should still suppose that Macaria probably possessed the better 'defence'. Would this necessarily be the case, however, if the battle was to take place in a jungle swamp where the tank's mobility and firepower would be the more severely hampered by the environment?

This example underlines the point that the simple purchase of weaponry is not a sufficient condition for the existence of 'defence'; the weapons must be appropriate to the form of warfare in which the nation expects to be engaged. The suitability of weaponry is also a factor in the peacetime state of deterrence. We might suppose, for example, that Macaria, if it were to concentrate its efforts on the construction of a 'Doomsday' weapon capable of global destruction, would have available far less 'defence' than Oceana with, say, conventional military forces, as it is extremely unlikely that the former will risk the use of *its* particular weapon for fear of self-destruction.

The obstacles to the deployment of weapons of high levels of sophistication may be political as well as purely strategic. This may be seen in more concrete terms by considering the cases of the involvement of the USA in Korea (1950–3) and Vietnam (1955–73). In purely military terms, the USA is possibly the strongest single nation on earth, accounting for some 25 per cent of global military spending. How then can we explain what Bose (1977) terms the 'Vietnamese paradox', namely that this particular nation got the better of a far more powerful rival, 'both in the battle-field and in the conference room'? Why did the USA not simply obliterate its enemies with the vast destructive power at its disposal?

Clearly, the reasons are complex, but we may note that, in spite of General MacArthur's protestation to the contrary, it did appear that there *was* a substitute for victory. In both of these cases, the USA was obliged to fight a 'limited' war for fear of antagonising any or all of three interest groups. First, massive escalation of military effort in either instance would have increased the probability of the USSR entering the conflict, involving the USA in a far more serious confrontation. Secondly, the USA's allies within the NATO became progressively more unconvinced of the validity of continued US involvement in these particular theatres (although their disapproval was felt more immediately in the case of Korea). Finally, and especially in the case of Vietnam, public opinion within the USA itself prevented all-out involvement and eventually obliged the US government to withdraw from that theatre altogether as the futility of limited warfare became all too apparent.

The purpose of these illustrations has been to dispel the myth that a low level of defence spending necessarily means a low level of security. Indeed, we have probably examined enough possibilities to suggest that military expenditure *per se* constitutes neither a necessary nor a sufficient condition for security, and we shall now go further to investigate the possibility that alterations to defence spending in ways which have been suggested might conceivably be accompanied by an increase in the security level of the nation concerned.

It is manifestly clear that, should the USA or the USSR wish to totally obliterate the average LDC, then the task could be easily accomplished from a technical point of view. Both of these nations possess sufficient nuclear firepower to wipe out all trace of such a nation's population and natural resources, a feat made possible by the LDC's lack of the appropriate weaponry to resist a ballistic missile attack.

This being the case, it is clear that, in some universal sense, we must consider such countries as Peru, Upper Volta and Burma as totally 'insecure', as they would immediately collapse in the face of such a nuclear attack. However, it is also abundantly clear that the reallocation of the entire national output of these LDCs towards the provision of a nuclear deterrent against the 'superpowers' would be quite inappropriate when we consider the range of economic, political and strategic reasons which make the possibility of such an attack so remote as to be nonistent. Prominent amongst these reasons which militate against such nuclear holocaust will be the desire of 'superpowers' to maintain the balance of power and the corresponding fear of conflict escalation to global level, the likely disapproval of such an action on the part of allies, and also the internal morality of the country concerned. Indeed, the recent past presents us with evidence of the 'superpowers' preferring to back down from conflicts, lose face or otherwise withdraw rather than risk the use of nuclear weapons to resolve the conflict by force – examples include the US withdrawal from Vietnam and the Soviet withdrawal from Cuba.

Having rejected this universal concept of insecurity, we now turn to the opposite end of the spectrum by suggesting that we certainly should consider Peru, Upper Volta and Burma to be specifically 'insecure' if they remained undefended from forms of conflict which are most likely to concern them. The experience of history suggests that such conflicts will be territorial.

Since 1945, all conflicts involving substantial commitments of economic resources to the war effort have occurred in the Third World region and such conflicts basically fall into one or more of three distinct categories. First, two of the most prodigious wars (Korea and Vietnam) have involved LDCs in conflict with the developed world (represented in these cases by the USA). Secondly, we have seen numerous intra-Third World conflicts involving nations of a roughly equivalent development status; the major examples here are the Middle East and India/Pakistan. Finally, several conflicts have taken place *within* particular LDCs themselves, as in the cases of Nigeria (1966–9), Ethiopia and the Philippines (throughout the 1970s).

In virtually all of these post-war conflicts, the control over, or the occupation of, enemy territory has been the primary concern of the aggressors – the USA was anxious to precipitate the invasion of Vietnam to forestall the spread of communism in South East Asia; ever since 1948, Israel has been concerned to establish a homeland in the Middle East at the expense of the Arab world; Nigeria was concerned to retain national integrity in the face of Biafra's attempts to establish self-government over a portion of Nigerian territory. In many respects, the outbreaks of these wars are unsurprising. Ever since the Second World War and even before, the drawing-up of international boundaries appears to have been a particularly arbitrary procedure, with little attention seemingly being paid to ethnic and cultural considerations. Present-day national boundaries in the Third World are frequently the legacy of colonial rule – ex-British and ex-French West Africa and

India/Pakistan/Bangladesh – or are the result of the partition of natio
occupied after the end of the Second World War – Korea and Vietnan
With the attainment of independence and the departure of the imperi
or occupying power, it is inevitable that the indigenous population wi
attempt to restructure those boundaries which have been imposed fro
outside. Any such restructuring must naturally occur at the expense
at least one other nation and this state of affairs can precipitate (ar
indeed frequently has precipitated) armed conflicts.

Even if the position of national boundaries is acceptable to a
concerned, many LDCs fear invasion for an additional reason whic
relates to their particular endowments of natural resources. At t
present time, the most important resource in question is oil, and t
expanding defence budgets of oil-states such as Kuwait, Bahrain ar
Iran may be taken in part as a reflection of a growing concern for t
security of their resources which are becoming increasingly short
supply. The theory that war is fought principally for economic reason
that is, country A will attack country B to gain control over the latter
resources, is by no means modern in origin. Plato was certainly convince
by it and it forms a cornerstone of the Marxist theory of imperialisr
Even twentieth-century liberal theorists such as Robbins (193
acknowledge the economic basis of international conflict whilst denyi
that such imperialism is immanent in capitalist develop
ment.

If the most likely threat to an LDC is therefore going to be the thre
of invasion to usurp resources (or a threat of internal succession for t
same purpose), what military strategy should be adopted to count
such a threat? According to a number of theorists, the most effecti
policy for a nation to adopt would be a particular body of tactics know
by a variety of names, which we shall for convenience collectively ter
'non-military defence' (NMD). As we shall see, this particular strateg
is a logical consequence for a military sector organised along intergr
tionist lines.

As Boserup and Mack (1974) have shown in their study of NM
it is only relatively recently that such a strategy has been thought
as anything other than 'downright subversive' or idealistic. The chan
in attitudes is due to a great extent to the lessons of the Vietname
war – first, the fact that material superiority may be insufficient to w
wars; secondly, a strategy based on the 'political mobilisation of t
people' can 'exhaust a professional military machine'; thirdly, wars c
be won by the generation of discontent amongst the civilian populati
of the invading nation.

Despite the name, NMD does possess a military side, although the operations of it are essentially interrelated with the role of civilians in the defence against invasion. At a completely non-violent level, civilian NMD will take the form of 'symbolic activities', such as demonstrations and strikes, which provide the invaders with a clear picture of civil feelings and also serve the important purpose of uniting the invaded nation. From a more active point of view, civilians may also engage in sabotage or terrorist activities to weaken the enemy's resolve.

The primary function of civilians, however, will be to support the armed forces against resistance and eventual counter-attack. In the case of invasions of the past, evidence suggests that the most effective form of armed resistance against conventional weaponry is guerrilla warfare. The objective of guerrilla strategy against an enemy possessing material superiority is to force confrontations in situations where the guerrillas' natural advantages may be used to the full, these advantages being mobility, knowledge of local conditions and, most important, the support of the civilian population. In the past, typical guerrilla tactics have included overextending the invader and cutting off his lines of supply, the exhaustion of the enemy by continual tactical retreat coupled with sporadic and rapid strikes, and the use of propaganda to demoralise both the invading army and also the electorate back home which is paying for it.

It is clear that the organisation of NMD is neither the province of the military nor of the civilians alone – the activities of both must be co-ordinated and pre-planned. In fact, NMD logically entails the gradual breakdown of barriers of interest between these two groups because, in order to provide resistance of maximum effectiveness, neither can function without the assistance of the other. In a very broad sense, therefore, NMD implies the politicisation of the military and the militarisation of the polity, to form the integrationist systems whose operations we have already studied.

In the context of NMD, several important points must be emphasised. First, NMD and socio-military integration do not, of necessity, imply a reduction in the quantity of defence expenditure in a nation's budget. This is because the military budget simply represents accounting costs and not the full social costs. To illustrate the point, suppose that, instead of sitting in a barrack-block all day, an army decides to involve itself in a village education programme. Military accounting costs would rise owing to, say, the purchase of teaching equipment, but it would be a social welfare benefit which would accrue. In other words, accounting costs may rise but net social economic costs will fall.

Secondly, there is also no necessity for the quantity of defence offered by 'formal' armed forces to fall, although this may of course take place. In simplistic terms, NMD might say that an army plus a civil population is strategically superior to an army in isolation. Additionally, the guerrilla theories of Mao Tse-tung and Vo Nguyen Giap stress the importance of conventional weaponry in the counter-offensive against a demoralised opponent.

Thirdly, NMD is a strategy of defence like any other in the sense that it is not really meant to be used as such! It is, rather, a strategy of deterrence, designed to suggest to would-be aggressors that the costs of invasion would be high, the war protracted and the outcome unfavourable to themselves. NMD must therefore achieve credibility in the same way as any other deterrence system. The techniques employed are a subtle form of national advertising and may vary from periodic shows of strength, as in the case of the USSR's famous military parades through the streets of Moscow, to actual 'low-level' conflicts to dissuade potential aggressors, such as China's attack on India in 1962. At this stage, we do not possess sufficient evidence to discover whether or not integration and NMD do actually deter, as few nations have so far tried out these techniques; all that we can say is that China has not yet been invaded and the Americans did withdraw from Vietnam! To this extent, however, NMD is no different from any other deterrence system which can only be tested by not being tested.

Throughout this work, we have assumed that the essential purpose of an armed force was the defence of national sovereignty and our arguments have been addressed to accomplishing this at minimum cost. From an economics point of view, we have accordingly derived a set of policy recommendations which nations 'ought' to implement in order to achieve our desired goals. We possess ample evidence, however, to realise that the objective we set ourselves is not the objective of all nations, either in the Third World or amongst the DCs. In certain cases, we have seen the goals of particular nations as the complete opposite, namely, conquest rather than defence. The rationale for aggression is complex indeed and may take on a variety of forms, from simple material greed to appeals to 'national destiny' which evoke memories of the Arabian *jihad* or even Smith's belief in 'civilising barbarians'. Suffice it to say that the economic calculus for an offensive strategy will include very different items from the one which we have been studying, and the optimum defence burden in this case will be completely different. The precise calculations will, of course, be specific to the particular action being contemplated; and, as we made clear at the beginning of the study, we are concerned with the economics of defence and not the economics of war.

Secondly, and because our model of integration implies a degree of civil consensus, we are unlikely to find NMD being considered by nations in which there exists social conflict. In particular, we should not expect to find integrationist policies being adopted in those countries in which the political and economic elite uses its military forces for the sole purpose of the repression, and the enforcing of the exploitation, of the mass of the population.

What, then, are the necessary conditions for integration? First, the military forces must be willing to 'deprofessionalise' and to contribute to the civil sector of the economy. Correspondingly, the civilian population must be willing to adopt a more positive role towards defence and to break down military/civilian barriers from the civilian side. Amongst other things, this involves the civilian regarding the soldier less as a person who is paid to 'do the defending' and more as the practitioner of a particular skill in an overall defensive team.

Clearly, such attitudes can only be fostered in a situation of political consensus and security. As we have seen, several LDCs already possess these conditions and have embarked upon integrationist policies of one variety or another. Other countries, such as Nigeria and Ghana, where the military rulers appear to be prepared to hand over power to civilian governments, also seem to possess them, although the position is not yet sufficiently clear to tell whether such policies could be successfully adopted in these countries.

This book began by presenting the fundamental economic problem, that resources devoted to defence cannot be employed elsewhere. Let us conclude by looking at a very simple public sector trade-off which underlines the central point at issue. We first met this trade-off in Chapter 2, namely, the more that is spent on defence, then the less will there be available for health care and social welfare programmes, other things remaining equal. Consider the following cases.[1]

In the Philippines in 1974, some 15,000 persons died violently, of whom perhaps one-half were killed in civil disturbances. Primarily as a result of these disturbances, annual military expenditure has more than quadrupled since 1972, whilst the armed forces have tripled in size. On the health front, however, the statistics paint a different picture. In the same year, 28,000 persons died of tuberculosis, 46,000 from pneumonia and 13,000 from nutritional deficiencies, diseases all of which are associated with poor living conditions, inadequate food and, in general, with poverty. In perhaps a more startling example, Egyptian war casualties in 1972 were, to take the World Health Organisation's most liberal estimate, around 11,000, in a year in which defence spending accounted for approximately 20 per cent of GNP. In the same year, nearly 250,000 Egyptians died of diseases of the respiratory and digestive systems. The moral is clear – guns kill in more ways than one.

Notes

1. Quotations from Smith (1873), Book 5, Chapter 1.1, pp. 289–97.
2. Russett (1966) discusses the ideological bias towards equilibrium theories in American social science.
3. The members of NATO are Belgium, Canada, Denmark, France, FR Germany, Greece, Italy, Luxembourg, Netherlands, Norway, Portugal, Turkey, UK, USA. The present members of the Warsaw Treaty Organisation are Bulgaria, Czechoslovakia, DR Germany, Hungary, Poland, Romania, USSR.
4. Data from UK Ministry of Overseas Development publicity leaflets, 1975.
5. Growth rates calculated from UN (1976a) Table 1; UN (1975a), Table 1, SIPRI (1977), Table 7A.1 and Table 7E.1

CHAPTER 2

1. Seventy per cent of Mexico's one-third of a million soldiers are part-time conscripts (IISS, 1977, p. 71).
2. For a survey of the statistical and conceptual problems in national income accounting, see Whynes (1974).
3. An example of such possible inconsistency arises with the Soviet Union, where adjustments have to be made to the rouble–dollar

153

exchange rate to yield a true picture of resource allocation. See IISS (1977), p. 11, for eight different estimates of Soviet defence spending. Because of its income conventions and lack of publication of data, Chinese information must also be regarded as 'approximate'.

4. SIPRI (1977), p. 222–3. The estimates of IISS given an even higher figure of some $370,000 million.

5. Third World regions are defined as follows: Middle East – Cyprus, Egypt, Iran, Iraq, Israel, Jordan, Kuwait, Lebanon, Saudi Arabia, Syria, Yemen (N. and S.); South Asia – Afghanistan, Bangladesh, India, Pakistan, Sri Lanka; Far East – Burma, Indonesia, Korea (N. and S.), Laos, Malaysia, Mongolia, Philippines, Singapore, Taiwan, Thailand, Vietnam (N. and S.); Africa – all nations in the African continent, *except* Egypt; Latin America – all nations in the Northern and Southern American continents, to the south of the USA.

6. Estimated from SIPRI (1977), p. 222–3.

7. Rapoport (1968), especially the introduction.

8. Aron (1958, 1966), Kahn (1960).

9. Monroe and Farrar-Hockley (1975), p. 5.

10. Bell's study of the African militaries in Van Doorn (1968), pp. 259–73.

11. Data from SIPRI (1972), pp. 92–3.

12. Data from UN (1971), p. 649.

13. For the Ghana coup, see First (1970) and Fitch and Oppenheimer (1966).

14. Kennedy (1974), p. 260.

15. IISS (1977), p. 47, gives a breakdown of South African weaponry and manpower.

16. Mahalanobis was a major contributor to the Indian Five-Year Plans (Hanson, 1966). A number of investment-orientated development theories are reviewed in Meier (1970), one of the most important being Lewis (1955).

17. Enthoven (1963) and Hitch (1965).

18. SIPRI (1977), pp. 222–3.

19. IISS (1972), p. 23. After colonial liberation and military coup the Portuguese Army now comprises 36,000 men in total (IISS, 1977, p. 27).

20. Baran and Sweezy (1968), pp. 178–183.

21. Gandhi (1971) reviews the empirical support for Wagner's Law in detail.

22. Lotz (1970), p. 134. Coefficients have been rounded; figures in brackets are *T*-ratios.
23. Data from Schwartz and Jasni (1958) and Holmans (1961).
24. Data from UN (1972), p. 662.

CHAPTER 3

1. For a comprehensive analysis of the spin-off of military technology to civil industry during the industrialisation of the UK, see Trebilcock (1969). For the effects of spin-off from the USA aerospace programme, see UN (1969a).
2. LDCs which currently manufacture major weapons are: Argentina, Brazil, Burma, Chile, China, Colombia, Dominican Republic, Egypt, Gabon, India, Indonesia, Iran, Israel, N. and S. Korea, Libya, Mexico, Pakistan, Philippines, Rhodesia, S. Africa, Syria, Taiwan, Thailand, S. Vietnam (Barnaby and Huisken, 1975, pp. 28–34).
3. The principal sources for this section are Dagli (1969) and SIPRI (1971), pp. 741–58.
4. SIPRI (1971), pp. 738–9. Other data in this section from SIPRI (1975a), pp. 292–3, SIPRI (1977), pp. 290–1 and 298–9.
5. Data for this section from IISS (1977), pp. 84–5.
6. Meier (1970), pp. 431–9, discusses the problems of labour absorption. Data also from this source.
7. This point is well brought out by Reynolds (1969) and also by Meier, loc. cit.
8. Data from IISS (1977).
9. Janowitz (1964), p. 76.
10. Lissak (1964) and Stifel (1972).
11. A review of sociological analyses of socio-economic development is presented by Hoselitz (in Hoselitz and Moore, 1963, pp. 11–31).
12. Op. cit. p. 128.
13. Data from (i) IISS (1977), (ii) USACDA (1972), (iii) SIPRI (1975) and UN (1971a).
14. The UN has presented several reports on disarmament and the adverse effects of defence spending; for example, UN (1972a).

CHAPTER 4

1. The data-source for US assistance is NACLA (1972), itself compiled from official US defence publications.
2. SIPRI (1975a), p. 221–2. The weaponry required by Iran was the 'Phantom' fighter aircraft, at that time the most powerful in the region.
3. For example, Hartley (1965).
4. Data for analysis from SIPRI (1971), pp. 880–1.
5. Eldridge (1969), pp. 163–71.
6. SIPRI (1971), pp. 691–702.
7. SIPRI (1971), pp. 144–5.

CHAPTER 5

1. Luttwak (1968), pp. 181–4; Finer (1975), p. 298.
2. UN (1971), p. 557. The principal sources for Ghana's armed forces and the coup are First (1970), Fitch and Oppenheimer (1966) and Pinkney (1972).
3. Polomka (1971), pp. 110–31.
4. UN (1971), p. 557.
5. IISS (1977), p. 59.
6. The middle classes are defined as those engaged in 'commerce, banking, insurance, or in technical, professional, managerial, administrative or clerical employments' (p. 1143).

CHAPTER 6

1. Hanning (1967), p. 28 *passim*.
2. Whitson (1972), pp. 215–27.
3. IISS (1977), pp. 52–4.
4. Yeh, in Yuan-li (1973), p. 483.

CHAPTER 7

1. Data on military spending from IISS (1972, 1977) and on deaths by various causes from the World Health Organisation (1976, 1977), *World Health Statistics Annual*.

Bibliography

Ahmad,K. U. (1972), *Breakup of Pakistan*, London: Social Science Publishers.
Allende, S. (1973), *Chile's Road to Socialism*, London: Penguin.
Aron, R. (1958), *On War*, London: Secker & Warburg.
Aron, R. (1966), *Peace and War*, London: Weidenfeld and Nicolson.
Arraes, M. (1972), *Brazil: The People and the Power*, London: Penguin.
Avineri, S. (1972), *Hegel's Theory of the Modern States*, Cambridge UP.
Baran, P. (1957), *The Political Economy of Growth*, New York: Monthly Review Press (quotations from the 1973 Penguin edition).
Baran, P., and P. Sweezy (1968), *Monopoly Capital*, London: Penguin.
Barber, W. F., and C. N. Ronning (1966), *Internal Security and Military Power – Counter-Insurgency and Civic Action in Latin America*, Ohio State UP.
Barnaby, F., and R. Huisken (1975), *Arms Uncontrolled*, Harvard UP.
Baylis, J., K. Booth, J. Garnett and P. Williams (1975), *Contemporary Strategy*, London: Croom Helm.
Benoit, E. (ed.) (1967), *Disarmament and World Economic Interdependence*, Columbia UP.
Benoit, E. (1973), *Defence and Economic Growth in Developing Countries*, Lexington: Lexington Books.
Benoit, E., and K. E. Boulding (eds.) (1963), *Disarmament and the Economy*, New York: Harper & Row.
Bolton, R. E. (1966), *Defense Purchases and Regional Growth*, Washington: Brookings Institution.
Bose, A. (1977), *Political Paradoxes and Puzzles*, Oxford: Clarendon Press.
Boserup, A., and A. Mack (1974), *War without Weapons*, London: Frances Pinter.

Brennan, D. G. (ed.) (1961), *Arms Control, Disarmament and National Security*, New York: Brazillier.

Brett, E. A. (1975), 'The Political Economy of General Amin', *Institute of Development Studies Bulletin* (University of Sussex), Vol. 7, No. 1.

Burt, R. (1975), *Defence Budgeting*, IISS Adelphi Paper, No. 112.

Christie, M. J. (1970), *The Simonstown Agreements*, Africa Bureau.

Cmnd 4521 (1970), *Supplementary Statement on Defence Policy*, HMSO.

Crozier, B. (ed.) (1972), *Annual of Power and Conflict*, London.

Cypher, J. (1974), 'Capitalist Planning and Military Expenditures', *Review of Radical Political Economics*, 6, 1–19.

Dagli, V. (ed.), (1969), *The Public Sector in India*, Bombay: Vora.

EIU (1963), *The Economic Effects of Disarmament*, London: EIU.

Eldridge, P. J. (1969), *The Politics of Foreign Aid in India*, London: Weidenfeld & Nicolson.

Enthoven, A. C. (1963), 'Economic Analysis in the Department of Defense', *American Economic Review*, 53, May Supplement, 413–23.

Finer, S. E. (1962), *The Man on Horseback*, London: Pall Mall.

Finer, S. E. (1975), 'The Mind of the Military', *New Society*, 7 August, pp. 297–9.

First, R. (1970), *The Barrel of a Gun*, London: Penguin.

Fitch, B., and M. Oppenheimer (1966), *Ghana, End of an Illusion*, New York: Monthly Review Press.

French, S., and T. A. Boyd (1971), *An Enquiry Concerning Employment Opportunities for Secondary School Leavers in Ghana*, University of Cape Coast; Social Studies Project, Research Report 6, Ghana.

Gandhi, V. P. (1971), 'Wagner's Law of Public Expenditures – Do Recent Cross-Section Studies Confirm it?', *Public Finance*, 26, 44–56.

Gutteridge, W. (1965), *Military Institutions and Power in the New States*, London: Pall Mall.

Hanning, H. (1967), *The Peaceful Uses of Military Forces*, New York: Praeger.

Hanson, A. H. (1966), *The Process of Planning*, Oxford UP.

Harbison, F., and C. F. Myers (eds.) (1965), *Manpower and Education*, New York: McGraw-Hill.

Hartley, K. (1965), 'The Learning Curve and its Applications to the Aircraft Industry', *Journal of Industrial Economics*, 13, 122–8.

Hartley, K. (1974), 'Programme Budgeting and the Economics of Defence', *Public Administration*, 52, 55–72.

Hayter, T. (1971), *Aid as Imperialism*, London: Penguin.

Hitch, C. J. (1965), *Decision-Making for Defense*, University of Carolina Press.

Hitchens, C. (1978), 'Two Dictatorships', *New Statesman*, 13 January, pp. 38–41.

Holmans, A. E. (1961), *United States Fiscal Policy, 1945–1959*, Oxford UP.

Hoselitz, B. F., and W. E. Moore (eds.) (1963), *Industrialisation and Society*, New York: Humanities Press.

Ianni, D. (1970), *Crisis in Brazil*, Columbia UP.

IISS (various dates) *The Military Balance*, London: IISS.

Jaguaribe, H. (1968), *Economic and Political Development*, Harvard UP.

Janowitz, M. (1964), *The Military in the Political Development of New Nations*, Chicago UP.

Johnson, J. J. (ed.) (1962), *The Role of the Military in Underdeveloped Countries*, Princeton UP

Kahn, H. (1960), *On Thermonuclear War*, Princeton UP.

Kende, I. (1972), *Local Wars in Asia, Africa and Latin America*, Studies on Developing Countries, No. 60, Budapest.

Kennedy, G. (1974), *The Military in the Third World*, London: Duckworth.

Kilson, M. (1963), 'African political change and the modernisation process', *Journal of Modern African Studies*, 1, 425–40.

Lee, J. M. (1969), *African Armies and Civil Order*, London: Chatto & Windus.

Lewis, W. A. (1955), *Theory of Economic Growth*, London: Allen & Unwin.

Lissak, M. (1964), 'Social change, mobilisation and the exchange of services between the military establishment and civil society – the Burmese case', *Economic Development and Cultural Change*, 13, 1–19.

Little, R. W. (ed.) (1971), *Handbook of Military Institutions*, Beverley Hills: Sage Publications.

Lofchie, M. F. (1972), 'The Uganda coup – class action by the military', *Journal of Modern African Studies*, 10, 19–35.

Loftus, J. E. (1968), *Latin American Defense Expenditures, 1936–1965*, Rand Corporation Memo, RM-5310-PR/ISA, California.

Lotz, J. R. (1970), 'Patterns of Government Spending in Developing Countries', *Manchester School*, 38, 119–44.

LPDSG (1977), *Sense about Defence*, London: Quartet.

Luttwak, E. (1968), *Coup d'état*, London: Allen Lane.

Martin, A., and W. A. Lewis (1956), 'Patterns of Public Revenue and Expenditure', *Manchester School*, 24, 203–44.

McNamara, R. S. (1968), *The Essence of Security*, London: Hodder & Stoughton.

McQueen, A. J. (1969), 'Unemployment and future orientations of Nigerian school-leavers', *Canadian Journal of African Studies*, 3, 441–61.

MEADP (1969), *The People's Plan for Progress*, Dar-es-Salaam.

Meier, G. M. (1970), *Leading Issues in Economic Development*, Oxford UP. (2nd ed.).

Monroe, E., and A. H. Farrar-Hockley (1975), *The Arab-Israel War, October 1973*, IISS Adelphi Paper No. 111.

NACLA (1972), *The U.S. Military Apparatus*, Berkeley and NY.

NEDC (1963), *Growth of the United Kingdom to 1966*, HMSO.

Nellis, J. R. (1972), *A Theory of Ideology*, Oxford UP.

Nordlinger, E. A. (1970), 'Soldiers in mufti', *American Political Science Review*, 64, 1131–48.

Nyerere, J. K. (1971), *Tanzania, ten years after independence*, Dar-es-Salaam.

Peacock, A. T., and J. Wiseman (1961) *The Growth of Public Expenditure in the United Kingdom* Princeton UP.

Peil, M. (1969), 'Unemployment in Tema – the plight of the skilled worker', *Canadian Journal of African Studies*, 3, 409–19.

Pinkney, R. (1972), *Ghana under military rule, 1966–69*, London: Methuen.

Polomka, P. (1971) *Indonesia since Sukarno*, London: Penguin.

Polomka, P. (1974), *Indonesia's Future and South-East Asia*, IISS Adelphi Paper 104.

Rapoport, A. (ed.) (1968), *Clausewitz – On War*, London: Penguin.

Reynolds, H. (1969), 'Economic development with surplus labor – some complications', *Oxford Economic Papers*, 21, 89–103.

Robbins, L. (1939), *The Economic Causes of War*, London: Jonathan Cape.

Robinson, J. (1970), *The Cultural Revolution in China*, London: Pelican.

Rose, H. and S. (1970), *Science and Society*, London: Pelican.

Rosen, S. (ed.) (1973), *Testing the Theory of the Military-Industrial Complex*, Lexington: Lexington Books.

Russett, C. E. (1966), *The Concept of Equilibrium in American Social Thought*, Yale UP.

162   *The Economics of Third World Military Expenditure*

Sahni, B. S. (ed.) (1972), *Public Expenditure Analysis*, Rotterdam UP.

Schwartz, C. F. and G. Jasni (1958), *U.S. Income and Output*, New York: US Department of Commerce.

SIPRI (1969, 1972, 1975, 1977), *World Armaments and Disarmament Yearbook*, Stockholm: Almquist & Wiksell.

SIPRI (1971 and 1975a), *The Arms Trade with the Third World*, Stockholm: Almquist & Wiksell (abridged edition, 1975, London: Pelican).

Smith, A. (1873), *Wealth of Nations*, London: Nelson.

Smith, R.P. (1977), 'Military expenditure and capitalism', *Cambridge Journal of Economics*, 1, 61–76.

Smith, W. E. (1973), *Nyerere of Tanzania*, London: Gollancz.

Stepan, A. (1971), *The Military in Politics*, Princeton UP.

Stifel, L. D. (1972), 'Burmese Socialism – Economic Problems of the First Decade', *Pacific Affairs*, 45, 60–74.

Taylor, A. J. P. (1963), *The First World War*, London: Hamish Hamilton.

Taylor, C. L., and M. C. Hudson (1972), *World Handbook of Political and Social Indicators*, Yale UP, 2nd ed.

Terrell, L. M. (1971), 'Societal stress, political instability and levels of military effort, *Journal of Conflict Resolution*, 15, 329–46.

de Tocqueville, A. (1961), *Democracy in America*, New York: Schocken Books.

Trebilcock, C. (1969), 'Spin-off in British economic history; armaments and technology', *Economic History Review*, 2nd series, XXII, p. 474–90.

UN (various dates), *Statistical Yearbook*, New York: UN.

UN (1969a), *Practical Benefits of Space Exploration*, New York: UN.

UN (1971a), *Yearbook of National Accounts Statistics*, New York: UN.

UN (1972a), *Economic and Social Consequences of the Arms Race and of Military Expenditure*, New York: UN.

UN (1975a), *World Demographic Yearbook, 1975*, New York: UN.

UN (1976a), *World Economic Survey, 1976*, New York: UN.

USACDA (1972), *World Military Expenditures 1971*, Washington: USACDA.

Van Doorn, J. (ed.) (1968), *Armed Forces and Society*, The Hague: Mouton.

Walinsky, L. J. (1962), *Economic Development of Burma, 1951–1960*, New York: Twentieth Century Fund.

Weidenbaum, M. L. (1964), *The Economics of Peacetime Defense*, New York: Praeger.

Weiss, S. J., and E. C. Gooding (1968), 'Estimation of differential multipliers in a small regional economy', *Land Economics*, 44, 235–44.

Whitson, W. W. (ed.) (1972), *The Military and Political Power in China in the 1970s*, New York: Praeger.

Whynes, D. K., (1974), 'The Measurement of Comparative Development – A Survey and Critique', *Journal of Modern African Studies*, 12, 89–107.

Windle, C., and T. R. Vallence (1962), 'Optimising Military Assistance Training', *World Politics*, 15, 91–107.

Withers, G. A. (1977), 'Armed Forces Recruitment in Great Britain', *Applied Economics*, 9, 289–306.

Yaun-li, Wu (1973), *China – A Handbook*, Newton Abbot: David & Charles.

Index